Freire and Feminism

FREIRE IN FOCUS

Series editors: Greg William Misiaszek and Carlos Alberto Torres

This series of short-format books provide readers a diverse range of Paulo Freire's work and Freireans' reinventions towards social justice both inside and outside education, without readers needing any prior knowledge of his scholarship. The books offer new perspectives on the work of Freire's teaching, ideas, methods, and philosophies. Each book will introduce Freire's work so it is easily understood by a wider audience without overly simplifying the depth of his scholarship.

Advisory Board

Ali Abdi; Marina Aparicio Barberán; Pep Aparicio Guadas; Michael Apple; Rima Apple; Ângela Antunes; N'Dri T. Assié-Lumumba; Oscar Azmitia Barranco; Lesley Bartlett; Kumari Beck; Tina Besley; ChenWei Chang; Luiza Cortesão; Regina Cortina; José Cossa; Sonia Couto; Eve Coxen; Pedro Demo; Jason Dorio; Anantha Duraiappah Mahatma; Liang Du; Gerald Faschingeder; Aslam Fataar; Moacir Gadotti; Chitra Golestani-Maghzi; Sandy Grande; Sondra Hale; Anne Harley; John Holst; Afzal Hossain India; Zhicheng Huang; Liz Jackson; Petar Jandric; Tony Jenkins; Aly Juma; Hyung Ryeol Kim; Sophie Kotanyi; Peter Lownds; Sheila Macrine; Peter Mayo; Lauren Misiaszek; Ernest Morrell; Raymond Morrow; Pedro Noguera; Maria del Pilar O'Cadiz; Irène Pereira; Michael Peters; Adriana Puiggrós; Jevdet Rexhepi; Saajidha Sader; Kabini Sanga; Ilse Schimpf-Herken; Daniel Schugurensky; Lynette Shultz; Graham Smith; Ana Steinbach Torres; Danilo Streck; Rebecca Tarlau; Massimiliano Tarozzi; António Teodoro; Spyros Themelis; Robert Tierney; Richard van Heertum; Yusef Waghid; Sung-Sang Yoo

Freire and Feminism

EDITED BY
EUNICE MACEDO

BLOOMSBURY ACADEMIC
LONDON · NEW YORK · OXFORD · NEW DELHI · SYDNEY

BLOOMSBURY ACADEMIC
Bloomsbury Publishing Plc
50 Bedford Square, London, WC1B 3DP, UK
1385 Broadway, New York, NY 10018, USA
29 Earlsfort Terrace, Dublin 2, Ireland

BLOOMSBURY, BLOOMSBURY ACADEMIC and the Diana logo are
trademarks of Bloomsbury Publishing Plc

First published in Great Britain 2025

Series design by Charlotte James
Cover image © Paulo Freire via Torres, Carlos Alberto (2014).
First Freire: Early writings in social justice education. Teachers College
Press. Background image © ilyast / Getty Images

ISBN: HB: 978-1-3504-7303-4
         PB: 978-1-3504-7304-1
       ePDF: 978-1-3504-7306-5
      eBook: 978-1-3504-7305-8

Series: Freire in Focus

Typeset by Integra Software Services Pvt. Ltd.
Printed and bound in Great Britain

To find out more about our authors and books visit www.bloomsbury.com
and sign up for our newsletters.

CONTENTS

FIRST WORDS

PART ONE Freire and Feminism(s) 13

PART TWO Pedagogy, Education, Body and Sexualities 45

FIGURES AND TABLES

Figures

Table

CONTRIBUTORS

Angelita Alice Jaeger is Associate Professor at the Center for Physical Education and Sports (CEFD) at the Federal University of Santa Maria (UFSM), Brazil. Since 1997, she has taught graduate and postgraduate courses in physical education. She leads the Diversity, Body, and Gender research group (GEDCG), where she advises qualitative research on body representations, gender relations and sexualities in different contexts of sports practices, focusing on studies on images and social networks. Angelita has authored articles and book chapters, the most recent being *The Women in Futsal Refereeing in Brazil* (2022).

Arilda Ines Miranda Ribeiro is Professor at the 'UniversIDADE' Program at the State University of Campinas and a member of the Historical, Geographical and Genealogical Institute of Campinas, Brazil. She holds a PhD in Philosophy and History of Education and retired as Full Professor of History of Education at São Paulo State University. She is a founding member of the Nucleus of Sexual Diversity in Education and the Research Group on Education, Culture, Memory, and Art. She researches and publishes in the history of education, gender and sexuality, including her book *The Education of Women in Colonial Brazil* (1997).

Elaine Gomes Ferro is Professor at the Federal University of Mato Grosso do Sul, Pantanal Campus, Brazil. She graduated from São Paulo State University with a degree in Pedagogy (2011), a master's degree (2014) and a doctorate (2023) in Education.

Grasiela Oliveira is a sports coach at the State Department of Education and Culture/Sergipe, Brazil. She taught physical education in schools for nineteen years and in universities for ten years, always committed to critical education. Currently, she works on organizing state and national sports competitions. She researches gender and sport with an investigative focus on martial arts.

Eunice Macedo is Assistant Professor at the Faculty of Psychology and Education Sciences, University of Porto, Portugal, and a full member of the faculty's Center for Research and Intervention in Education (CIIE), coordinating the research community of practice Inclusion and Voice Policies: Education, Gender and Intersectionality. Her research interests include the study of Paulo Freire and its relations with feminist thought and pedagogies, young adult citizenship with voice, education with the arts, early leaving from education and training, second chance education and gender. She has a wide range of publications within her research interests, the most recent in English being 'Making "The Best" of Private Education' (2020).

Jorge Luís Mazzeo Mariano was a pedagogue at São Paulo State University (UNESP) and had a master's degree from the Federal University of São Carlos, a PhD in Education from UNESP, and a postdoctoral position at the University of Western São Paulo, Brazil. Before his death, he directed the studies and research group History and Memories of Education, served as the coordinator of the Pedagogy course, and taught at the Graduate Program in Education at the Federal University of Mato Grosso do Sul. His research interests included the history of Brazilian education and the history of women.

Laura Fonseca is retired Professor at the Faculty of Psychology and Education Sciences, University of Porto, Portugal. Her research interests include sexualities, gender studies, femininities and masculinities, adolescent pregnancy, social justice, youth, cultures and education. She has been a researcher on projects such as TemRedE – Building Local Networking in Education? Decision-Makers' Discourses and Strategies on School Achievement and Drop-Out, and PIDOP – Processes Influencing Democratic Ownership and Participation. Her more recent publication in English is Fonseca, Laura, Helena C. Araújo and Sofia A. Santos (2012), 'Sexualities, Teenage Pregnancy and Educational Life Histories in Portugal: Experiencing Sexual Citizenship?', Gender and Education, 24 (6): 647–64.

María José Chisvert-Tarazona is Lecturer at the Department of Teaching Methods at the University of Valencia, Spain. She has a master's degree in social economy and a master of teacher training. She researches organizations dedicated to education, training for social and labour insertion, professional training and learning at work, with a special interest in vulnerable groups and the transitions between training and employment. She is a member of the Transitions Research Group (GIUV2013-093) https://www.uv.es/transicions. She has carried out research stays at universities in São Paulo (Brazil), Porto (Portugal), Catalonia and Seville (Spain).

Monica Riutort is Director of Family Services Peel Institute, Peel Institute of Research and Training. She has a Bachelor of Science from the University of Chile, a Bachelor of Arts in Sociology from York University, and a Master of Arts in Adult Education and Counseling Psychology from the University of Toronto. She provides strategic advice to management and develops innovative programs addressing equity from a framework of anti-oppression and anti-racism. She is a founding member of the International Society for Equity and recently completed a publication entitled 'New Roads to Anti-Racism Oppression and Equity' for the *International Diversity Journal*.

Nilma Renildes da Silva is Professor at São Paulo State University (UNESP), School of Sciences, Bauru, Brazil, in the Department of Psychology. She has a master's degree in Social Psychology and a PhD in Educational Psychology. Her research interests are within the historical-cultural perspective, focusing on gender violence, violence in schools, and other phenomena considering the intersectionality among gender, social class and race. She has published on gender studies and edited a book on the method of materialist historical-dialectical in Social Psychology (2005).

Paula Silva is Associate Professor at the Faculty of Sport, University of Porto (FADEUP), Portugal. Sports have been her passion from an early age, which led her to become a coach and physical education teacher at secondary schools for many years. Since 2005, she has taught graduate and postgraduate sports pedagogy and physical education teacher education courses. As a researcher at CIAFEL (Research Centre in Physical Activity, Health and Leisure), she focuses mainly on gender in sports and physical education. She authored 'Construction of Gender in Physical Education' (2007), book chapters and international articles.

Pilar Cambronero-García is a member of the technical staff at FOREM PV, a foundation for training and employment. She deals with the communication of the foundation, the Equality Plan and the Integrated Management System. She is also the founder of the LA CALLE BAILA Association, coordinating the project ¡A QUELAR!: of artistic creation through flamenco for boys and girls at risk of social exclusion.

Sandra Rupnarain is Executive Director at Family Services Peel Institute, Peel Institute of Research and Training, Mississauga, Ontario, Canada.

Sofia Almeida Santos is Research Fellow and Knowledge Broker at the Centre for Research and Intervention in Education (CIIE) of the University of Porto, Portugal. Between 2020 and 2022, she has been an Expert Adviser of the Cabinet of the Minister of Education. She has a European PhD (2015) in Educational Sciences in sex education and citizenship, gender and sexuality studies between Portugal and England (in partnership with Cambridge and Leeds University). As a member of CIIE since 2006, she has actively collaborated on several research projects, engaging in international mobilities (Warwick University), giving lectures and publishing in her fields of interest.

Sofia Marques da Silva is Associate Professor of the Faculty of Psychology and Educational Sciences at the University of Porto, Portugal, a member of the Centre for Research and Intervention in Education (CIIE), coordinating the research community of practice on Youth, Education, Diversity, and Innovation. Her research encompasses inclusion, diversity, and youth, young people from rural and border regions, publishing internationally and nationally. She is convenor of the European Conference on Educational Research (ECER); editor-in-chief of journal *Educação, Sociedade & Culturas*; vice president of the Portuguese Society of Education Sciences; member of the National Council of Education; and expert of EACEA (Education, Audiovisual and Culture Executive Agency).

Tânia Suely Antonelli Marcelino Brabo is Associate Professor in the Department of School Administration and Supervision at São Paulo State University (UNESP), Brazil. Her research interests focus on democratic management, human rights, gender, citizenship, and education. Her most recent book is *Democracia, Direitos Humanos, Gênero e Cidadania: Teoria, Políticas e Cotidiano das Escolas Públicas* [Democracy, Human Rights, Gender and Citizenship: Theory, Policies and Daily Life in Public Schools] (2022).

SERIES EDITOR'S FOREWORD

Feminism *with* Freire: Needs, Critiques, Limitations, and Possibilities

Greg William Misiaszek (Series Editor; Beijing Normal University (BNU), China, Faculty of Education (FoE), Institute of Educational Theories; Paulo Freire Institute, UCLA, USA) with Ji Eun Chung (BNU, FoE, Institute of International and Comparative Education, China)

Freire has had various critiques, some less substantial from those who have read his most famous book *Pedagogy of the Oppressed* (1970) in, we would argue with others (Au and Apple 2007; hooks 1993; Schugurensky 2011), non-critical, superficial ways and as though his writing and overall work stopped with its publication in the early 1970s. In various ways, ignoring the self-reinvention of Freire with his work counters understanding what humanizing *unfinishedness* is that he argued for in the book – the reinvention of the Self through *conscientization* (conscientização) – reinventing the essence of his most famous book's words to current, diverse contexts. However, there are more substantial critiques also, which frequently revolve around his work as not (more) focusing beyond socio-economic class issues – e.g. racism, gender, heteronormativity, and anti-environmentalism (beyond-humans domination).

This book is an excellent example of using Freire's words directly (especially well beyond *Pedagogy of the Oppressed*), reinventing his work through feminist lenses and more current contexts, and providing critiques and limitations of feminism and Freire's work. For those who might have preconceptions that Freire's and/or Freireans' work could not possibly add value to feminist approaches, we encourage you to read this short book. The reason could not be better worded than the following by the editor, Eunice Macedo, in the book's proposal wrote:

> feminist readers may be challenged to build new understandings of Paulo Freire and his work, which he himself described as feminist, and that may be inserted in a wave of humanist feminism in a horizon of *hope* and *possibility* crucial in the current and troubled time.

This book provides a wealth of feminist approaches to using and reinventing Freire to recognize and counter fatalism that is embedded in patriarchy and heteronormativity *with* intersectionalities of other socio-historical oppressions. For example, the intersectionalities of gender and race. Arguments for Freire's essentialness *with* feminism and race might be most famously emphasized by bell hooks (hooks, 1993, 2014). The first chapter by Macedo delves into hooks' arguments, and the book overall is a vital resource in understanding how Freire's work has influenced hooks' works, as well as (in)directly influencing feminism globally. Macedo highlights this by quoting hooks arguing that Freire's work 'allowed her [hooks] to cross the "impacts of race and class as factors that shape female identity"' (Macedo, Chapter 1, p. 15). For example, in her book *Teaching to Transgress: Education as the Practice of Freedom* (1994), hooks wrote about her usage of Freire to (re)develop relevant feminist pedagogies for multicultural contexts. Reinventing Freire's idea on the innate polity of education to disrupt the politics of othering systematically ignored in 'banking' approaches, hooks constructively criticizes and promotes Freire's work for further empowering feminist approaches to teaching and possible praxis from learning. While criticizing Freirean work as a 'phallocentric paradigm of liberation' as Macedo points out, hooks also supported his work, in part, for his unrelenting commitment to democracy and equity towards ending all forms of oppressions/domination. It should also be noted that hooks (1994) lends Freirean work to help highlight oppressions from the 'lives of poor black women' that were frequently not addressed by what she named as 'white bourgeois feminist theorist'.

Uniqueness of the book and its themes

This book is wonderfully placed within Bloomsbury's *Freire in Focus* short-length book series as the Series Editors Carlos Alberto Torres and myself (Greg) envisioned the books both introducing important societal, pedagogical topics for liberation and ending oppressions/domination *with* Freire. An undeniable strength is this book's diverse, widespread contextualization, delving into globally diverse locations, perspectives and happenings, but also deepening unpacking at local spheres. The modern contextualization of *Freirean and Feminism* by the chapters' authors' work diversifies the reading and rereading (i.e., Freirean literacy) of situations of vulnerability and inequality as inseparable from the larger, often purposely hidden systems of oppressions/domination. The authors challenge readers to (re)analyse how patriarchy, nuanced with other critical lenses, misrepresents gender 'differences' with numerous microaggressions from local-to-global spheres, including, but far from all-inclusive, curricula, the media (i.e., informal education, public pedagogy), governing and governance, academia and sports.

We read three overall themes throughout the book; however, this is very generalized and only represents our readings of this richly diverse book. First is the restating somewhat the book's strengths mentioned in the paragraph above. In short, the reinventing, or 'transferring' as named in da Silva's chapter, of Freire's pedagogical practices, theories and philosophies onto a wide range of contemporarily relevant issues. This book widens the applicability of Freirean work *with* feminism within the current contexts – but with nuanced and intersectional approaches. For instance, the book explores women's sports in mixed martial arts (MMA) to challenge gender norms, emphasizing the tensions of binary and biologized representations (specifically gender reductionism [see Hanson, 1994]). Another example is exploring how cinematic language, such as in the movie *Precious*,[1] can help capture transformative possibilities of education towards women's liberation in various ways.

Second, the authors provide in-depth dialogue between Freirean and feminist work, especially within short-length chapters. The authors' collective writing styles, in which Eunice Macedo stressed how this book developed, can be witnessed in the dialectic-structured chapters. Some chapters delve deeply into problematizing the sexist language and patriarchal groundings often evident in Freire's work. Authors give various feminist critiques, especially against Freire's earlier work and the possibilities of adding a vast array of gender issues to his work. Some authors also discuss how feminist approaches deepened Freire's critical reflexivity on a wide array of gender inequality issues. In doing so, the authors raise the importance of language and linguistics in reproducing stereotypes of 'men' being *the* universal model of the subject, which was intentionally revised by Freire in his later works (see Chapter 2). The chapters touch upon hidden language and lack of recognition that can reinforce the system of (in)visible oppression – i.e., the microaggressions of patriarchal language and linguistics. For instance, some authors focus on arguing that schooling has become heteronormalizing spaces through hidden sex curricula. Throughout, the book provides nuanced portrayals of Freire with very substantial critique (as defined previously).

Third and lastly, the book is saturated by the chapter authors' experiences to call for Freire with feminist (de/re) constructions of teaching. In numerous ways, this book calls for teaching and methodological conscientization in examining the readers' Self – resulting in autobiographic/auto-ethnographic critical re-readings. Many of the chapters can be read as such (paradigm shifting) (re)reading. Many authors (in) directly argue for experiences to be sources of knowledge and learning for emancipation and liberation praxis – coinciding, partially, with feminist standpoint theories. By presenting autobiographical pieces, the authors illustrate how experiences can/must be used to reveal largely systematically hidden structures of (un)just power and the (mis)taught patriarchal, heteronormative ideologies that further entrench and intensify oppressions.

Note

1   https://www.imdb.com/title/tt0929632/.

References

Au, W. W. and M. W. Apple (2007), 'Reviewing Policy: Freire, Critical Education, and the Environmental Crisis', *Educational Policy*, 21 (3): 457–70.

Freire, P. (1970), *Pedagogy of the Oppressed*, New York: Herder and Herder.

Hanson, B. G. (1994), 'Beyond "Biologizing": The Unit Question in Gender Analysis of Senile Dementia in Families', *International Journal of Sociology of the Family*, 24 (2): 57–68. Retrieved from http://www.jstor.org/stable/23028653.

hooks, b. (1993), 'bell hooks Speaking about Paulo Freire – The Man, His Work', in P. Leonard and P. McLaren (eds), *Paulo Freire: A Critical Encounter*, 145–52, New York: Routledge.

hooks, b. (1994), *Teaching to Transgress: Education as the Practice of Freedom*, New York: Routledge.

hooks, b. (2014), *Talking Back: Thinking Feminist, Thinking Black* (New edition), New York: Routledge.

Schugurensky, D. (2011), *Paulo Freire*, London: Bloomsbury.

ACKNOWLEDGEMENTS

The Portuguese government also supports this work through the Foundation for Science and Technology, IP (FCT) under the multi-year funding awarded to CIIE (grants no. UIDB/00167/2020 and UIDP/00167/2020).

First Words

The Explanatory Power of Paulo Freire's Fundamental Thinking

Sofia Marques da Silva

CIIE – Centre for Research and Intervention in Education of the Faculty of Psychology and Education Sciences, University of Porto, Portugal[1]

Freire, a founding author of educational thought, developed his theoretical and analytical proposals from feminist thinkers, particularly creating the ground for broad discussion and giving space for critical perspectives. That open space allowed reinterpretations and approaches by authors from different scientific fields, as in many contributions found in this book. However, the broadness of his theoretical model, as Freire acknowledges, allowed his theories to be paradoxically appropriated by oppressive systems (Freire [1992] 2012).

Paulo Freire's thought or, as Ribeiro and colleagues name it in this volume, 'the analytical appropriation' of Freire, is perhaps used since this thinker is clear and solid in his arguments; these characteristics have allowed those who study

Freire to carry out or propose knowledge transfer to fields that are often not the founding context of his theory, constructed on the field of critical pedagogy.

Returning to Paulo Freire seems equally related to the persistent search for social justice, echoing the transformative potential of his proposal. The possibility of continued analysis of the structure of inequalities that reinforce the place of vulnerability for specific populations, where the option for subjectivation and participation is diminished, is a viable epistemological reason to keep discussing Freire. Since the question of vulnerability, as ontology, is transversal to his thought, it is also why, in this book, many reflections return to it, such as the contribution by Chrisvert-Tarazone and Cambronero-Gracía (see Chapter three, in this volume).

Deriving from philosophy, **ontology** questions the meanings of existence, being, becoming, reality and so forth – the value of values.

Freire's relevance is also grounded on the proposal of a systemic analysis of his object, oppression, avoiding a fragmented analytical exercise. This book, edited by Eunice Macedo, with its diversity of contributions, focuses on structural dimensions of Freire's thought, such as social transformation, autonomy, social justice, equality, freedom, practice and reflection. This exercise of revisiting Freire's perspectives is done through the specific interest of the authors who seek, above all, to understand the processes that may, in different contexts, contribute to weakening or resisting the strength of structures, mainly when it enhances the combination of inequalities that has placed women, and other minorities, in a 'citizenship of subalternity' (Araújo 2007: 164).

Freire's proposal is a warning against the illusion of transparency. It compels us to be constantly reflexive, evaluating our positions and questioning our practices, including research and educational practices.

As this volume shows, the Freirean approach has revealed strength and resistance but also opportunities to be contested and challenged in its explanatory power. Gleaning and appropriating Freire also seem to strengthen his central approach's explanatory possibility. Paulo Freire is, in fact, a founding author who, as she mentions, drawing on bell hooks, questions but does not abandon himself (see Macedo, Chapter 1 in this volume, with details on bell hooks).

bell hooks is the name adopted by **Gloria Jean Watkins** (1952–2021), an award-winning African American radical feminist who studied with Paulo Freire and focused on the discussion of ethnicity and gender in her work. In particular, her book *Teaching to Transgress: Education as the Practice of Freedom* (1994) brings to the fore the influence of Freire in her thought.

Freire's proposal has resistance because the social problems that gave rise to his analysis are persistent, but in other guises, possibly more liquid (Bauman 2001) and, for this reason too, more difficult to detect and combat. On the other hand, Freire proposes an approach between experiences and the construction of educational thinking, bringing radical proposals for the levelling of powers and the hierarchization of knowledge in the pedagogical relationship.

liquid modernities move from a view of rigidity and fixedness to a view of fluidity (like water). That means the move from the great unchangeable structural social and historically ascribed narratives (such as family, state and religion) to the more individualized/group realities and the plurality of meanings that families, states and religions may assume within a view of diversity and mutability.

Freire does not seem to be afraid to label his work, recognize the sexist language in his early writings and critically analyse its enunciative place (Geraldi 2005). Freire recognized many arguments from feminist thinkers, a perspective that can be found in several contributions in this volume, such as that of Brabo and Macedo, providing a systematic account of the different positions towards Freire and his work.

Recognizing that Freire's theoretical framework is valid for continuing the critical interpretation of social and educational issues implies a healthy negotiation of theoretical and methodological understandings. The contributions presented here are an example of such negotiation, this being the condition for the expansion of the theory itself. In this alignment, the negotiation process can also contribute to theoretical and methodological decolonization (Silva 2016).

The epistemological value of Freire's thought is under discussion (Altamirano 2016; Vassallo 2012), including some forgetfulness of his work in the Global North and South. Altamirano, in an article entitled 'Where Is Paulo Freire?', considers him to be a precursor of the epistemologies of the South later developed by Boaventura de Sousa Santos (in several works), who, according to her, also seems to have forgotten Freire.

Epistemologies of the South is a (contested) notion that refers to the recognition of knowledge of social groups in conditions of vulnerability as a form of resistance against the systematic injustices and oppressions caused by capitalism, colonialism and patriarchy.

Authors such as Raymond Morrow and Carlos Alberto Torres (1998: 137) have affirmed the advantage of placing Freire's work in a broader context of analysis of 'different constellations of domination and dialogue' being 'seen as an approach originally developed on the margins of Latin

America, influenced by European and North American social theory, which it later also came to influence'. It is thus from a counter-hegemonic place that Freire elaborates the proposal to actively analyse constructed situations of oppression from places of power.

Science has offered representations/constructions of dominant realities that condition subjects to perform their identity construction, taking this offer as a reference. Science produces legitimated, filtered and surveilled knowledge (Silva 2016), constituting a language. It is impossible to conceal how it has contributed to the reproduction of dominant and imperative worldviews and the silencing of other speeches and proposals. Sandra Harding (1991) asked about the possibility of using science for liberating purposes when it is aligned with Western, bourgeois and masculine projects.

While we may be as pessimistic as Bauman when he considers that 'intellectuals have never really trusted their powers to transform the world of flesh and blood' (2008: 210), we can, however, acknowledge the non-neutrality of our standpoint (Harding 2003) and follow England's (1994) proposal by reflecting on the way we research. For introspection and analysis of the researcher self, 'reflexivity is critical to fieldwork; it induces self-discovery and can lead to insights and new hypotheses about the research questions' (82).

Therefore, we produce situated knowledge from perspectives located in a particular place, allowing us to foster more emancipatory and socially committed knowledge (Haraway 1988). This is even more evident in the autobiographical approach in the contribution of Ribeiro, Mariano and Ferro, which closes this book. If we think of research as a practice embedded in a field of forces (Bourdieu 2004) that aligns dominant cultures, in particular through a dominant language and exercising powers of action, we find the root of numerous invisibilities that are naturalized. As Bourdieu states, science, especially its legitimacy and legitimate use, is a permanent motive of struggle in the social world.

This way of interpreting others as if they were on the other side prevents us from seeing situations of vulnerability and inequality as part of a larger system of domination. In her chapter in this book and other works (Fonseca 2001, 2009), Laura Fonseca places much of her reflection on social justice. The invisibility of certain historical processes and the organic nature of social realities construct an idea of stagnation of certain subjects and their history. Freire's subject is the protagonist of their movement when they become aware of the omission to which they are condemned in the powerful discourse. In the process of conscientization, this subject does not make its way alone but in a dialogical action in which, according to Freire, different subjects share the same plan without objectifying others. On the other hand, the action of subjects is facilitated when preference is given to knowledge that ensures the participation of social groups involved in research or intervention projects (B. S. Santos 2009). In this alignment, the value of experience has become central in the social sciences and humanities and education sciences in particular, implying a paradigmatic and methodological shift. Fonseca's contribution to Freire's approximation exercise focuses on experience, a fundamental concept in Paulo Freire's pedagogical proposal, recognizing the value of experience as conscientization.

Resistance or discomfort also grows as an opportunity for change (Silva, Jaeger and Oliveira, in this book). Through the example of the body of women in sport – as a context of participation – these authors show how a place is made in an arena in which others have played, socially and historically. From this contribution, we can also discuss how the idea has been disseminated that women are the artisans of their own bodies (Bauman 1999). The governance of the body, namely through sexuality as a device of social control (Ramos, in this volume; S. A. Santos, Fonseca and Araújo 2012), has been the motive for movements, contestation and resistance. In analysing a film as a cultural repository, Chrisvert-Tarazona and Cambronero-García also show how female characters create places of resistance and claim and struggle for dignity. It is, therefore, through education that transformation is made possible, and this transformation can only take place with empowered subjects and equivalent, equitable, and fair conditions of participation and voice. However, as Chisvert-Tarazona and Cambronero-García point out (in this volume), the empowerment narrative is intertwined with oppression.

Social transformation is one of the most cherished aspects of Freire's proposal, perhaps for the optimistic sense it carries (Ribeiro and colleagues, in this volume), but possibly also for its radical sense (Fonseca, in this volume). The optimistic aspect associated with its radical character is where the impulse arises when, in certain contexts, we are more unaccompanied in the struggle for the equality of difference and human dignity. Freire's radical proposal is not divorced from his models of rupture. The social paradigm change based on critical education does not happen through continuity but through ruptures (Kuhn 1983). It is done, above all, in the presence of the Other who acts on the world and in the strong interaction between reflection and social practice.

As the concerns of the chapter presented by Sofia A. Santos in this book show, how can we intentionally address these debates and their object to the younger generations? Freire has been an undeniable reference. He makes us responsible for knowing the subjects of education, particularly their values and the involvement in intersubjective educational dynamics, as Freire argues, configuring a dialogic system.

Awakening consciences through education implies questioning the *status quo* and inequalities. In other words, the critical positions must go beyond specific problems to move on to the analysis and confrontation with the structures at their origin, denaturalizing oppression (Riutort and Rupnarain; Silva, in this volume). In their discussion of violence, these authors place the struggle for women's emancipation within the class struggle based on the dynamics of the social structure. Educational work invests in reinterpreting the phenomena of inequality to better understand and act upon them.

Learning and teaching to question, as emphasized in the work *For a Pedagogy of the Question* (Freire and Faundez 2002), also serve for students to exercise self-criticism and understand themselves located in a certain place, while at the same time questioning the set of processes that marks this positionality. As Freire ([1996] 2003: 54) states in *Pedagogy of Autonomy*, '[M]y presence in the world is not that of one who adapts to it, but of one who is part of it. It is the position of those who struggle not only to be objects of history but also subjects.'[2]

It is also relevant to emphasize the value that school and school knowledge, powerful knowledge (Young 2007), has represented on the path to citizenship and autonomy of women, an aspect pointed out, particularly by Ribeiro, Mariano and Ferro in this work. The value attributed by Freire to the knowledge of the subjects, their experiences and the meaning of education based on references familiar to them is not in opposition to the value of school or its liberating potential.

Following the reflections of Ribeiro, Mariano and Ferro (in this volume), it is difficult to understand a curriculum that represents a policy of knowledge yet does not integrate a real project of emancipation. A universalist and supposedly neutral perspective of the curriculum explicitly or implicitly validates forms of segregation and perpetuation of stereotypes and processes of subordination of certain forms of knowledge (Santos and Meneses 2009).

As Chisvert-Tarazona and Cambronero-García discuss (in this volume), school culture, including dominant knowledge, selected and transmitted as universal, is the culture of dominant groups. Knowledge, transmitted as a banking act (Freire [1968] 2003), according to the Freirean perspective, constitutes 'something which exists outside and independently of the people involved in the pedagogical act' (Silva 2005: 209). That knowledge, legitimated by a general epistemology, does not authorize other types of knowledge or the conversation between them. In school, as in other social contexts, we have witnessed what Riutort and Rupnarain (in this volume) call culturally incompetent approaches.

We return to Freire, whose thinking is based on respect for the knowledge of the world produced through language by weaker and oppressed groups and the value of this knowledge for constructing valid identities. Because language is a critique and repositioning of Freire, language and discussing what we mean when we say something are central. Yet, it is still undervalued concerning gender, especially women, by academia, education and thinkers who see themselves in a Freirean school of thought and are close to his pedagogical model. By considering language as an insignificant form of the struggle for equality, the structure of inequality is maintained through the most powerful representation and production of the same and the other. Regarding equality, men and women should be included in the discussion (Azambuja et al. 2013), and these must be treated as human rights issues.

Through Freire, we understand the specifics of the issues and how they fit into a global framework. Addressing these issues goes beyond the scope of microanalysis and promotes the possibility of critique and decoding. The struggle against contexts and processes of oppression affects the way we allow oppression and inequality, especially concerning women, to be represented in curricula and other school texts, in politics, the media and academia.

The different chapters, written from different positions, including geographical ones (Herr and Anderson 2005), contribute to the re-encounter with Paulo Freire so that the reader can also interpret aspects that are both local and integrated into a global system that produces injustices. Different authors in this work point out aspects related to what Soja (2010) calls unjust geographies, namely how science has treated the Global South and its scientific production, especially the thinking of Paulo Freire, which has been silenced (Altamirano 2016).

We can also highlight the plurality of voices that Riutort and Rupnarain point out in this volume and the need for certain voices to be heard differently (Macedo 2012). This means that the interpretation of inequalities implies the consideration of socio-economic and geographic dimensions but also the intersection (Crenshaw 1991) with ethnicity, gender, generation, sexuality, etc., to the extent that differences take on particular configurations that depend on the articulation of different and contextualized forms of discrimination.

Apart from what has been pointed out, which is mainly due to how I have understood the authors' choices in dialogue with Freire, this book's contributions help answer the inevitable question: 'What can an author do?' The diversity of the contributions represents a reflective engagement with Freire's thought, with each author contributing their readings and appropriations but also ensuring that other directions of understanding are highlighted. Thus, this book is not only a historical look at the break in the construction of inequalities and the structure of oppression. Above all, it reminds us of the fragility of the rights and opportunities that have been won and of others that remain to be secured. In this sense, research is responsible not only to advance knowledge but also to be a partner for social change and a life of dignity. As we all know, one of the most difficult global challenges is how we can collectively maintain a critical consciousness and the possibility of open dialogue.

Notes

1   Acknowledgements: This work is also supported by the
     Portuguese government, through the Foundation for
     Science and Technology, IP (FCT), under the multi-year
     funding awarded to CIIE (grants no. UIDB/00167/2020 and
     UIDP/00167/2020).
2   Translated from the original: 'minha presença no mundo não
     é a de quem a ele se adapta, mas a de quem nele se insere. É a
     posição de quem luta para não ser apenas objeto, mas sujeito
     também da História' (Freire [1996] 2003: 54).

References

Altamirano, A. F.-A. (2016), 'Where Is Paulo Freire', *The International Gazette*, 78 (7): 677–83.

Araújo, H. C. (2007), 'Políticas da Diferença e Cidadania na nossa Formação', *Educação, Temas e Problemas*, 3 (2): 159–68.

Azambuja, M., C. Nogueira, S. Neves and J. M. Oliveira (2013), 'Gender Violence in Portugal: Discourses, Knowledge and Practices', *Indian Journal of Gender Studies*, 20 (1): 31–50.

Bauman, Z. (1999), *Modernidade e Ambivalência*, Rio de Janeiro: Jorge Zahar.

Bauman, Z. (2001), *Modernidade Líquida*, Rio de Janeiro: Jorge Zahar.

Bauman, Z. (2008), *Medo Líquido*, Rio de Janeiro: Jorge Zahar.

Bourdieu, P. (2004), *Para Uma Sociologia da Ciência*, Lisboa: Edições, 70.

Crenshaw, K. (1991), 'Mapping the Margins: Intersectionality, Identity Politics, and Violence against Women of Color', *Stanford Law Review*, 43 (6): 1241–99.

England, K. (1994), 'Getting Personal: Reflexivity, Positionality, and Feminist Research', *The Professional Geographer*, 46 (1): 80–9.

Fonseca, L. (2001), *Culturas Juvenis, Percursos Femininos, Experiências e Subjectividades na Educação de Raparigas*, Oeiras: Celta.

Fonseca, L. (2009), *Justiça Social e Educação: Vozes, Silêncios e Ruídos na Educação Escolar de Raparigas Ciganas e Payas*, Porto: Afrontamento.

Freire, P. ([1968] 2003), *Pedagogia do Oprimido*, Rio de Janeiro: Paz e Terra.

Freire, P. ([1992] 2012), *Pedagogia da Esperança: Um Reencontro com a Pedagogia do Oprimido*, Rio de Janeiro: Paz e Terra.

Freire, P. ([1996] 2003), *Pedagogia da Autonomia: Saberes Necessários à Prática Educativa*, São Paulo: Paz e Terra.

Freire, P. and A. Faundez (2002), *Por uma Pedagogia da Pergunta*, Rio de Janeiro: Paz e Terra.

Geraldi, J. W. (2005), 'A Linguagem em Paulo Freire', *Educação, Sociedade & Culturas*, (23): 7–20.

Haraway, D. (1988), 'Situated Knowledge: The Science Question in Feminism as a Site of Discourse on the Privilege of Partial Perspective', *Feminist Studies*, 14 (3): 575–99.

Harding, S. (1991), *Whose Science? Whose Knowledge? Thinking from Women's Lives*, Ithaca, NY: Cornell University Press.

Harding, S. (2003), *The Feminist Standpoint Theory Reader: Intellectual and Political Controversies*, London: Routledge.

Herr, K. and G. L. Anderson (2005), *The Action Research Dissertation: A Guide for Students and Faculty*, Thousand Oaks, CA: Sage.

Kuhn, T. (1983), *La Structure des Révolutions Scientifiques*, Paris: Flammarion.

Macedo, E. (2012), 'Reconstructing Femininities and Masculinities: Northern Portuguese Students Speak about Their Lives, Desires, and Dreams', *Educação, Sociedade & Culturas*, (35): 66–88.

Morrow, R. A. and C. A. Torres (1998), 'Jürgen Habermas, Paulo Freire e a Pedagogia Crítica: Novas Orientações para a Educação Comparada', *Revista Educação, Sociedade & Culturas*, (10): 123–55.

Santos, B. S. (2009), 'Para Além do Pensamento Abissal: Das Linhas Globais a uma Ecologia de Saberes', in B. S. Santos and M. P. Meneses (eds), *Epistemologias do Sul*, 23–71, Coimbra: Almedina/CES.

Santos, B. S. and M. P. Meneses (2009), *Epistemologias do Sul*, Coimbra: Almedina/CES.

Santos, S. A., L. Fonseca and H. C. Araújo (2012), 'Sex Education and the Views of Young People on Gender and Sexuality in Portuguese Schools', *Educação, Sociedade & Culturas*, (35): 29–44.

Silva, S. M. (2016), 'Multi-Sited Ethnography of Young People's Educational Mobilities: Methodological, Epistemic and Cognitive Decolonisation', paper presented at European Conference on Educational Research, Dublin, 22–6 August.

Silva, T. T. (2005), 'Pedagogia do Oprimido versus Pedagogia dos Conteúdos', *Educação, Sociedade & Culturas*, (23): 207–14.

Soja, E. W. (2010), *Seeking Spatial Justice*, Minneapolis, MN: University of Minnesota Press.

Vassallo, S. (2012), 'Critical Pedagogy and Neoliberalism: Concerns with Teaching Self-Regulated Learning', *Studies in Philosophy and Education*, 32 (6): 563–80.

Young, M. (2007), 'Para que servem as escolas?', *Educação e Sociedade*, 28 (101): 1287–302.

PART ONE

Freire and Feminism(s)

CHAPTER ONE

Freire and Feminism(s): From Resistance to Recognition within the *Milieu*

Eunice Macedo

CIIE – Centre for Research and Intervention in Education of the Faculty of Psychology and Education Sciences, University of Porto, Portugal[1]

Paulo Freire has been recognized as one of the greatest pedagogues of the twentieth century. His thoughts, actions and scientific production were constructed in a dialectical relationship with the world of life and its people, including a large group of intellectuals with whom he discusses and builds his work. Author of an enormous diversity of pieces, some solo and others in dialogue, his work has inspired educators worldwide, giving rise to a creative Freirean movement in defence of liberation through education. Freire upholds the utopia of another viable world guided by humanization, ethics, aesthetics and solidary relations.

The **aesthetics** we are talking about here refer to the construction of a sensitive and respectful relationship with the world and other people. Hence, **aesthetics** goes beyond its most common sense: the definition of a set of principles concerned with the nature and appreciation of beauty.

In addition to the broad reflection on education, Freire has been recognized for his 'method' of literacy. More than a syllabic, analytical and synthetic method of learning to read and write, the 'method' is based on generative themes articulated with the cultures and realities of the learners, constituting a process of awareness for a transforming social action. To this end, the 'method' – intended to teach illiterate adults to read and write in 30 to 40 hours – is based on thematic research, thematization (coding/decoding), and reading and writing. Guided by strong political beliefs, the 'method' distances itself from SESI's welfare-oriented vision that tried to circumvent class conflicts (as referred by Freire in several works). Hence, the 'method' is based on conscientization. This process goes beyond the awareness of extreme situations of oppression that inform individual lives of concrete subjects to mobilize learners in a dialogical movement of transitive consciousness as subjects inserted in specific social groups, which, in turn, can lead to a critical, transformative consciousness of oneself and these contexts (Macedo et al. 2013).

Transitive consciousness is an intermediate moment in the process of conscientization in which people understand that they are not alone in suffering specific forms of oppression. This means people move away from a magical, ahistorical view of the world (real consciousness) to understand the historicity of oppression, even if in a simplistic way, which will allow them to move further to develop a higher level of consciousness (critical consciousness) engaged with change.

> **C**onscientization is a socio-historical process that builds on dialogue within concrete social circumstances and that fosters people's move from oppressed objects to liberated subjects able to act and transform their realities.

When I recently revisited the book edited by Peter McLaren, Peter Leonard and Moacir Gadotti (1998), *Paulo Freire: Poder, Desejo e Memórias da Libertação* (Power, Desire and Memories of Liberation), I was particularly enthused by Freire's assertion, despite the feminist critique of his work, 'I have learned a lot from feminism and have come to define my work as feminist, seeing feminism as closely related to the process of self-reflection and political action on behalf of human liberation'[2] (Freire and Macedo 1998: 204). Inspired by this statement, which is controversial at the least, I decided to explore the conceptual vein of the relationships between Freirianism and feminism (Macedo 2017, 2021, 2022).[3] Constructed in critical pedagogy, Freirianism and feminism may be seen as *epistemological and methodological emancipatory traditions of voice* (Arnot 2006). They are concerned about eliciting the silenced voices and investing in social change. The first departs from social class and the second from gender. They both expand their conceptual scope by including other dimensions of inequality: gender and 'race' in the first case and socio-economic in the second. In education, both traditions are expressed in liberating pedagogies that: (i) reconceptualize the relationship between teachers and learners (in a double role); (ii) work towards the empowerment of teachers and learners; (iii) value their voice(s), including the multiplicity of structural locations of power that inform it (gender, class, 'race', etc.); and hence (iv) challenge the conventional notions of pedagogy. This chapter departs from the discussion of feminist criticism to Freire to reflect upon Freire's commitment to social justice, the construction of a language of resistance within a horizon of liberation, and the recognition of analogies between

Freirianism and feminism beyond *time and place*, as part of the *emancipatory traditions* in education.

Discussing feminist critiques of Freire's work

As a theoretical current and political movement (Magalhães, Pinto and Tavares 2003), feminism has been analysed in different waves, with different objectives, different moments of emergence and temporal overlaps. In the 1970s, feminist criticisms of Freirean thought were expressed, such as the sexism of language and the patriarchal vision, which can be located within the scope of a second wave of feminism. This wave asserted itself between the 1960s and 1980s, with other social movements that called for equality and difference and renegotiated the 'value of hierarchies of values and power' (Nogueira and Silva 2003: 13).

In the 1990s, defending feminist critical literacy and representational politics, Jeanne Brady (1994) contested Freire's work, alleging his reluctance to address the multiple, complex and contradictory meanings inherent to human subjectivity in dialogic processes, including the lack of conceptualization of the specific oppression and subjectivity of women. In her words, this was evident in Freire's first works in both the use of sexist language and the view of 'reproduction' as merely linked to the economy, a position that does not equate to women's reproductive work in the family. This is an idea on which Marxism and feminism conflict.

Like Weiler and other feminist thinkers, bell hooks (1994: 49) focuses on the absence of gender concerns and the presence of sexist language in Freire's early writings, which 'build a phallocentric paradigm of liberation' common among leaders, politicians, intellectuals, progressive critical thinkers, of the time, 'in which the symbol of liberation and the experience of patriarchal masculinity [...] [were] always linked as if they were the same'; a paradigm that, as she states, would place women in subordination. In the same vein, other authors recognize the value of Freire's theorization of oppression and the pedagogy of the oppressed while emphasizing the absence of gender and sexuality and the patriarchal view in Freire's arguments.

> A **paradigm** is a standard perspective or set of ideas that inform the way one looks at something. The principles in a **phallocentric paradigm** are seen as deriving from the phallus (or penis) as a symbol of male dominance.

Kathleen Weiler (1991, 1996, 2002a, 2002b, 2004) is one of Freire's staunchest critics. A lack of questioning of the gender divide in the public and private spheres and of women's concerns; a lack of response to feminist criticism; 'generalizations and universalism' that would allow the application of Freire's thought to any situation of oppression, despite the patriarchal perspective of women's subordination to the domestic space (Weiler 2002a); universalization of the 'oppressed', which hides individual differences, replicating 'societal arrangements of power' in classrooms (20); devaluation of the feminist movement, by hiding the different lines of thought within it; and, still, an inability to understand 'the patriarchal privilege' inherent in his comments about women (Weiler 2002b: 83); as well as Freire's assertion as a woman, as a failed attempt to 'overcome the phallocentric logic of the West' (86) constitute the most pressing criticisms.

The assumptions of male privilege in Freire's thought are particularly explored in the essay *Rereading Paulo Freire* (Weiler 2002b) within the tradition of feminist pedagogy. Recognizing that Freire, along with Foucault and Dewey, is one of the male authors most referred to by feminist researchers, Weiler attributes this to the passionate style of Freire's prose and his commitment to social justice and human rights. In her view, identifying women with the Freirean 'oppressed' can lead to homogenizing women and concealing other forms of oppression inherent to the privileges of 'race' and class, among others, which I would say implies an intersectional approach. However, as I see it, Freire's so-called *passionate style* can be associated with a more flexible and dialectical rationality that fostered the emergence of 'new figures to occupy the cosmos humanly and communally' (Henriques 2003: 133). As this philosopher states, this rationality constitutes a human form of knowledge with affection, embraced by many feminists. Thus, it allows a rupture with the (re)production of Cartesian knowledge, in which reason and emotion are erroneously dissociated (Damásio 2000), and *reason* – seen as equal in all men [*sic*] – arose as the foundation of the democratic ideal (Rodis-Lewis 1979). This perspective is still present in the contemporary scientific production subsidiary of a positivist paradigm of supposed objectivity.

From Descartes' philosophy, Cartesian **knowledge** builds on the divide between mind and corporeal body. Hence, **Cartesians** argue that deductive reasoning is at the roots of scientific knowledge, which builds on *a priori* 'innate ideas'.

Later, Weiler (2004) resumes the criticism of the masculine bias in Freire's theorization, as well as of the principles of universality, in both feminism and Freirianism, which, as she says, do not encompass the specificities of individual lives, neither the contradictions between oppressed groups in conflict nor the position as oppressed in one sphere and privileged or oppressor in another. The author seems unaware that Freire ([1968]1981), in the *Pedagogy of the Oppressed*, stated that the oppressed contained the oppressor – the worker, oppressed at work, could constitute himself as an oppressor in the family.[4] Having accused Freire of generalizing about feminism, in this assertion, Weiler does not seem to consider the different 'feminisms' within feminist theory. Radical feminism, socialist and Black feminism (Macedo 2003) are some examples that show that the feminist theory goes beyond linearity as it builds on complexity (Nogueira and Silva 2003).

Josephine Donovan (1989) also established analogies between Freire's proposal and feminist awareness-raising practices based on the same Marxist premises in constructing a group identity and a sense of solidarity. Like Freire's work, socialist feminism has a Marxist basis, however rejecting the idea of gender equality in Marxist theory despite the sexual division of labour. Such a view must be challenged in the face of the male right to property and their assumption of supremacy and power in the family (Nóbrega and Santos 2003). Admittedly, socialist feminism tends to combine the best of Marxism and radical feminism, seeking to resolve women's subordination in the public and private spheres (Bryson 1992) and overcome cleavage points in classical Marxism that contributed to the reproduction of inequalities.

> **M**arxism – from Marx – is a political philosophy of analysis of society and the economy that explains class relations and social conflict as deriving from the economy. Social transformation is seen as directly related to change in the economic relations of power between social classes.

Commitment to social justice, rights and a language of resistance

With regard to social justice, a concept underlying the ideal of human liberation, transversal to Freirianism, it is worth mentioning Freire's (1993) remarkable work *Professora Sim,*

Tia Não: Cartas a Quem Ousa Ensinar (Teacher, not Aunt: Letters to Those Who Dare Teach), in which the author resists the idea of *mothering* that would have justified the women's teaching profession. Arguing that such a profession requires commitment, militancy and professional specificity, Freire claims professional dignity for women as citizens with rights – subjects, authors and actors of their own history. Thus, by refusing to identify the female teacher with an aunt, he seeks both to avoid a distorted view of the female teacher's professional task and 'to uncover the ideological shadow resting, slyly in the intimacy of false identification. Identifying a female teacher with an aunt [...] is like proclaiming that teachers, like good aunts, shouldn't fight, shouldn't rebel, shouldn't go on strike' (Freire 1993: 12).

This bridges Freire's commitment to social justice, human rights and feminist concerns in mutual conceptual interpellation. Both veins can be inserted in the framework of the emancipatory traditions of voice (Arnot 2006), with Freire's as a critical sociology of silenced voices, with social class as a starting point. Notably, Freire ([1968] 1981) emphasizes that the dialogical educational praxis of conscientization allows deviation from a 'culture of silence' to a political consciousness, acquired through the development of critical thinking and translated into the ability to name – and change – the world.

> **P**raxis refers to the human 'reflection and action upon the world in order to transform it' as described by Freire (1972: 52), in the book *Pedagogy of the Oppressed*.

Other possible dialogues with feminist authors can be highlighted. This is the case of Iris Young (1990), who identifies premises for a global citizenship centred on justice and appeals to ideals of social justice (Young 2000) that correspond to general conditions of injustice: oppression and domination, respectively, institutional constraints to self-development and self-determination; Laura Fonseca (2009) who combines social justice and school education, focusing on girls' voice; Ruth Lister (1997, 2007) who announces a universally differentiated citizenship capable of welcoming universal human rights and human diversity; Dina Kiwan (2005) who combines citizenship and human rights, decentring from the relationship with the state; Madeleine Arnot (2009) who discusses youth citizenship and the role of education in citizenship with a focus on human rights and gender; and Helena Araújo (2009) who discusses the visibility of citizenship in the analysis of educational contexts attentive to human rights and inclusion, in terms of *redistribution*, *recognition* and *participation*.

Beyond time and place...

As a representative of a liberating thought emerging from Latin America (Donoso Romo 2020), the work of Freire flows beyond time and space. However, quite rightly, Weiler (2004) defends the need to read Freire's work in the light of the epochal context of the neo-colonialist and imperialist political and economic situation of world development. It is worth mentioning that Freire ([1968] 1981) already emphasized the relevance of epochal/contextual dimension, characterizing an epochal unit as the set of ideas, conceptions, hopes, doubts and values seeking fullness in dialectical interaction under specific challenges. Hence, the transformation of the world is a political act that forms the generational dimension of historical processes in the dialectic between dreams and counter-dreams. These dimensions involve different views of reality, group and class interests, prejudices, and ideological constructions perpetuating the contradiction between past and present (Freire 2000).

> The neocolonialist and imperialist view implies the (more or less subtle) imposition as universal of the values and culture of dominant states/groups on a given society/group. The prevalence of these effects on ex-colonized lives is called neocolonialism.

The view of education as a liberating political act, as in the *Pedagogy of the Oppressed*, is dear to feminist thinkers, who stand on the latter in favour of the liberation of women and other groups in subordination. In *Ain't I a Woman: Black Women and Feminism*, hooks (2014) highlights the passage from object to subject at the root of Freirianism, as illustrated.

hooks shows the adhesion to Freire's rhetoric and its commitment to democracy and equity in the face of feminist educational goals of liberation. Weiler (2002b) admits this feminist move despite needing a new language and new feminist imagery. The work of hooks is exemplary in this matter. Despite Freire's allocation to a 'phallocentric paradigm of liberation' (hooks 1994: 49), she highlights the need to constructively criticize Freire's work and learn from his liberating view in the framework of empowering feminist thought. The reflection, based on Freire, allowed her to cross the 'impacts of race and class as factors that shape female identity' (53), taking the debate beyond the borders of the United States. Furthermore, hooks (1994) emphasizes that more than the 'white bourgeois feminist theorists' in privileged positions (see also Macedo 2003), Freire recognizes the subordination and greater vulnerability to the forces of oppression of the most disadvantaged people, allowing an understanding of the 'lives of poor black women'.

Particularly inspired by Freire, in *Teaching to Transgress: Education as the Practice of Freedom*, bell hooks (1994) develops a relevant feminist pedagogy for multicultural contexts, guided by the intersectionality of class, race and gender. This formulation takes advantage of Freire's conceptualization of a liberating, problematizing, humanizing

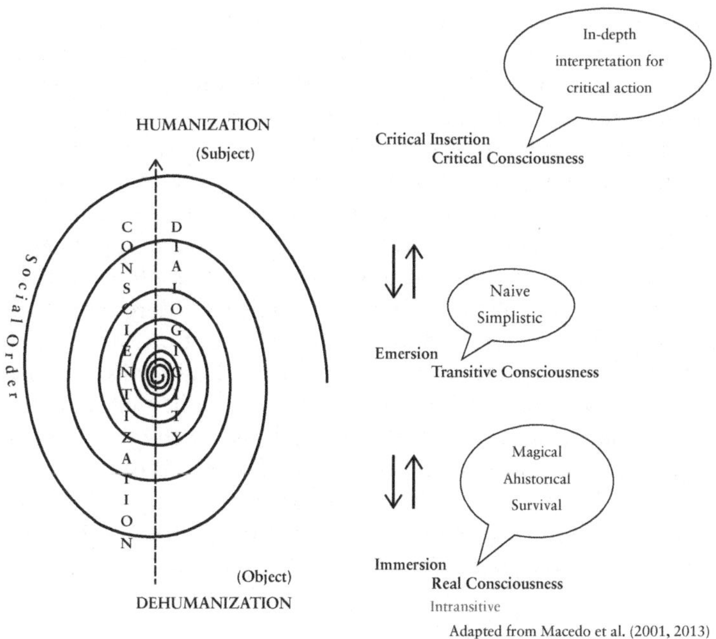

FIGURE 1.1 *Conscientization in Freire: Moving from object to subject.*

education based on the practice of freedom. This constitutes
an education supported by discovery and reflection on the
experiential worlds of the students and appeals to their active
participation in the construction of knowledge. To that extent,
affirming the *politicity* of education, hooks allies with Freire
to deviate from 'banking education', which inculcates norms
and normalizes these worlds under a socio-ideological and
historical-cultural model based on oppression and the denial
of the 'other'. This 'other' – the passive and unaware learner
– receives pre-selected and finished knowledge, like an empty
vault where valid knowledge is deposited.

Despite her resistance, Weiler (2004) positively combines
feminist and Freirean pedagogies under common assumptions
in the face of oppression, consciousness and historical change.

Both approaches focus on oppression as a material condition of life and defend conscientization as a political action to overcome dominant discourses; both are committed to justice in an outlook of liberation, seeing human beings as actors of their own history. In turn, bell hooks emphasizes convergences in the weaving between Freire's proposal and the 'living pedagogy' of many people and some Black teachers, invested with a liberating mission against 'racism and white supremacy', which builds her 'thought about the art of teaching' (hooks 1994: 46). And Koning (2005) establishes interconnections between Freire's philosophy of conscientization of concrete subjects in concrete contexts and Rosi Braidotti's feminist philosophy, which affirms the need for a 'policy of time and place' that defines the experience and goes through a 'loss of unity' and the 'fragmentation' of the Subject–Woman in her multiple belongings. This can be seen as an appeal to the diversity of dimensions of oppression that match subordination in women and that call for transformation.

> **Racism and white supremacy** build on the erroneous belief that the lighter-skinned, or 'white', human races are of greater value than other racial groups, just because of their skin color. Ultranationalist, racist and fascist groups have embraced and tried to disseminate this exclusionary view of the world that has no respect for human diversity.

Final remarks

Throughout this text, I likened and discussed feminist critiques of Freire while finding similarities and distances between approaches. If feminists and *Freirianists* are united in the search for liberation, they clearly have different starting points, the former of gender, the latter of social class, two dimensions that generate inequality and that, along with others such as race and ethnicity, demand urgent resolution, as shown by the demands of Black feminism represented by bell hooks.

This debate brought to the fore the Freirean view of the possibility of reflection and action to transform the world as actors and authors of our history. It also presented the hope of contributing to emphasizing the value of mobilizing the common features of these two emancipatory traditions rather than building on what separates them – a horizon of liberation that builds on commonalities without veiling the specificities of feminism, and Freirianism seems unprecedented and viable, today and in the future.

It is not for me, nor for the reader, to decide on the statement made by Freire, as a feminist, within a framework of legitimate self-nomination. However, his assertion seems justified in his own terms. Self-reflection and political action on behalf of human liberation, about feminism(s) and Freirianism, can be reinforced in their combination and mutual interpellation as feminist Freirianism or Freirean feminism, in line with their departing points, to shelter human rights and the diversity that enriches the human species.

Notes

1   Acknowledgements: This work is also supported by the Portuguese government, through the Foundation for Science and Technology, IP (FCT), under the multi-year funding awarded to CIIE (grants no. UIDB/00167/2020 and UIDP/00167/2020).

2   Free translation.

3   Even if Freire himself criticized the 'isms', I introduce the term *Freirianism* to refer to the liberation movement of educators worldwide who reinvent the work of Paulo Freire with a view to social justice and humanization, assuming our roles of transformative subjects and authors of our history.

4   Macedo (2009) argues that elite young people in a situation of economic privilege can contain 'the oppressed' as they learn to 'be an oppressor' by means of the naturalization of

social inequalities through socialization processes in which recontextualization is almost absent, given the coincidence between aspects of the school environment and other contemporary environments.

References

Araújo, H. C. (2009), 'Prefácio', in E. Macedo (ed), *Cidadania em Confronto: Educação de Elites em Tempo de Globalização*, 9–10, Porto: CIIE/Livpsic.

Arnot, M. (2006), 'Gender Voices in the Classroom', in C. Skelton, B. Francis and L. Smulyan (eds), *Sage Handbook on Gender and Education*, 407–22, London: Sage.

Arnot, M. (2009), *Educating the Gendered Citizen: Sociological Engagements with National and Global Agendas*, London: Routledge.

Brady, J. (1994), 'Critical Literacy, Feminism and a Politics of Representation', in P. Mclaren and C. Lankshear (eds), *Politics of Liberation: Paths from Freire*, 142–53, New York: Routledge.

Bryson, V. (1992), *Feminist Political Theory: An Introduction*, London: Palgrave Macmillan.

Damásio, A. R. (2000), *O Erro de Descartes: Emoção, Razão e Cérebro Humano*, Sintra: Publicações Europa-América.

Dewey, J. (1938), *Experience & Education*, New York: Kappa Delta Pi.

Donoso Romo, A. (2020), *A Educação Emancipatória: Iván Illich, Paulo Freire, Ernesto Guevara e o Pensamento Latino-Americano*, São Paulo: Universidade de São Paulo.

Donovan, J. (1989), 'Radical Feminist Criticism', in J. Donovan (ed), *Feminist Literary Criticism: Explorations in Theory*, ix–xxi, Lexington, KY: The University Press of Kentucky.

Fonseca, L. (2009), *Justiça Social e Educação: Vozes Silêncios e Ruídos na Educação Escolar das Raparigas*, Porto: Afrontamento.

Freire, P. ([1968] 1981), *Pedagogia do Oprimido*, Rio de Janeiro: Paz e Terra.

Freire, P. (1972), *Pedagogy of the Oppressed*, London: Penguin.

Freire, P. (1993), *Professora Sim, Tia Não: Cartas a Quem Ousa Ensinar*, São Paulo: Olho d'Água.

Freire, P. (2000), *Pedagogia da Indignação: Cartas Pedagógicas e Outros Escritos*, São Paulo: UNESP (FEU).

Freire, P. and D. Macedo (1998), 'Um Diálogo com Paulo Freire', in P. McLaren, P. Leonard and M. Gadotti (eds), *Paulo Freire: Poder, Desejo e Memórias da Libertação*, 203–10, Porto Alegre: ArtMed.

Henriques, F. (2003), 'As Teias da Razão: A Racionalidade Hermenêutica e o Feminismo', in M. L. Ferreira (ed), *As Teias que as Mulheres Tecem*, 133–44, Lisboa: Colibri.

hooks, b. (1994), *Teaching to Transgress: Education as the Practice of Freedom*, New York: Routledge.

hooks, b. (2014), *Ain't I a Woman: Black Women and Feminism*, New York: Routledge.

Kiwan, D. (2005), 'Human Rights and Citizenship: An Unjustifiable Conflation?', *Journal of Philosophy of Education*, 39 (1): 37–50.

Koning, M. (2005), *Lugares Emergentes do Sujeito-Mulher: Viagem com Paulo Freire e Maria de Lourdes Pintasilgo*, Porto: Afrontamento.

Lister, R. (1997), *Citizenship: Feminist Perspectives*, New York: New York University Press.

Lister, R. (2007), 'Inclusive Citizenship: Realizing the Potential', *Citizenship Studies*, 11 (1): 49–61.

Macedo, E. (2003), 'Enraizamentos e Vozes para os Feminismos Negros', in C. Marques, C. Nogueira, M. J. Magalhães and S. Silva (eds), *Um Olhar sobre os Feminismos*, 125–50, Porto: UMAR.

Macedo, E. (2009), *Cidadania em Confronto: Educação de Jovens Elites em Tempo de Globalização*, Porto: LivPsic, CIIE.

Macedo, E. (2017), 'Paulo Freire, um Pensador Feminista? (Re) Articulando Conceitos e Debates', in E. Macedo (ed), *Ecos de Freire e o Pensamento Feminista: Diálogos e Esclarecimentos*, 23–58, Porto: LivPsic, IPFP, CRPF, CIIE.

Macedo, E. (2021), 'Pedagogia Freiriana e Pedagogias Feministas: (Des)Encontros e Diálogos (Im)Possíveis?', *Ideação*, 23 (1): 202–22.

Macedo, E. (2022), 'Pedagogia Freiriana e Pedagogia Femminista: Come "Tradizioni Emancipatrici della Voce"', *Rivista MeTis*, (6): 79–92.

Macedo, E., Vasconcelos, L., Evans, M., Lacerda, M., & Vaz Pinto, M. (2013), *Revisitando Paulo Freire: Sentidos na educação*, Brasília: Liber Livro.

Magalhães, M. J., T. Pinto and M. Tavares (2003), 'Os Feminismos e a UMAR: Uma Reflexão a Propósito de "Aprofundar a Democracia no Mundo da Vida"', in C. Marques, C. Nogueira, M. J. Magalhães and S. Silva (eds), *Um Olhar sobre os Feminismos*, 19–30, Porto: UMAR.

McLaren, P., P. Leonard and M. Gadotti, eds (1998), *Paulo Freire: Poder, Desejo e Memórias da Libertação*, Porto Alegre: ArtMed.

Nóbrega, L. and E. Santos (2003), 'Feminismo Marxista/ Socialista', in C. Marques, C. Nogueira, M. J. Magalhães and S. Silva (eds), *Um Olhar sobre os Feminismos*, 31–45, Porto: UMAR.

Nogueira, C. and S. Silva (2003), 'Introdução', in C. Marques, C. Nogueira, M. J. Magalhães and S. Silva (eds), *Um Olhar sobre os Feminismos*, 9–18, Porto: UMAR.

Rodis-Lewis, G. (1979), *Descartes e o Racionalismo*, Porto: Rés Editora.

Weiler, K. (1991), 'Freire and a Feminist Pedagogy of Difference', *Harvard Educational Review*, 61 (4): 449–74.

Weiler, K. (1996), 'Myths of Paulo Freire', *Educational Theory*, 46 (3): 353–71.

Weiler, K. (2002a), 'Introduction', in K. Weiler (ed), *Feminist Engagements: Reading, Resisting, and Revisioning Male Theorists in Education and Cultural Studies*, 1–12, New York and London: Routledge.

Weiler, K. (2002b), 'Rereading Paulo Freire', in K. Weiler (ed), *Feminist Engagements: Reading, Resisting, and Revisioning Male Theorists in Education and Cultural Studies*, 67–87, New York and London: Routledge.

Weiler, K. (2004), 'Freire e uma Pedagogia Feminista da Diferença', *Ex aequo*, (8): 91–111.

Young, I. (1990), *Justice and the Politics of Difference*, Princeton, NJ: Princeton University Press.

Young, I. (2000), *Inclusion and Democracy*, Oxford: Oxford University Press.

CHAPTER TWO

Encounters between Paulo Freire and Feminisms

Tânia Suely Antonelli

Marcelino Brabo

Introduction

The reflections proposed by this chapter are permeated by the defence of Paulo Freire's theoretical and political vigour for discussing feminist causes in contemporary times. The ideas of this Brazilian education theorist and educator are based on the libertarian and transformational consciousness that motivated and continues to motivate social movements, including feminists, emphasizing that feminism also contributed to deepening critical reflection on gender inequality in the work of Paulo Freire.

Initially, we will provide a brief history of feminism in Brazil, from its first manifestations until the 1960s–1970s, followed by the presentation of Freire's work in the same period, when he faced feminist criticism. His ideas reflect the possibilities of social change towards humanization, combined with the meanings he ascribed to the conceptions of dialogue in a critical and political formation.

The feminist movement in Brazil: Through the historical path until the 1970s

As a visible social movement, feminism manifested in the second half of the twentieth century. Feminist struggles started from recognizing women's oppression and asserting the relationships between men and women as socially, culturally and politically transformed and not inscribed in nature. Historically, the feminist movement experienced moments that are called *waves*. According to Fougeyrollas-Schwebel (2009), Pedro (2005) and Pinto (2003), among others, *first-wave* feminism developed at the end of the nineteenth century. It was centred on the call for political rights – such as the right to vote and be elected – and social and economic rights – such as paid work, study, property and inheritance.

According to the same authors, *second-wave* feminism emerged after the Second World War and prioritized women's right to own their bodies and pleasure, and against patriarchy, understood as the power of men in the subordination of women. At that time, the banner that the *private is political* was defended to hold the state responsible, especially in what concerned violence against women in the domestic sphere.

These feminist and women's movements began to gain visibility in the 1960s in the United States. As the literature points out, the text by Betty Friedan, *The Feminine Mystique*, published in 1963, and the work of Simone de Beauvoir, *The Second Sex*, in France in 1949, contributed to strengthening the feminist movement in those countries, also influencing Brazil.

> Consciously or not, the **androcentric view** places the masculine point of view at the centre of one's world, culture and history, thereby culturally. This view does not take femininity into account and marginalizes it. Taken as universal, the male is seen as the human model to be followed.

At the beginning of the *second–wave* feminist movement, the word *gender* was absent. The concern with language, as a subtle way of reinforcing the androcentric view of the world, begins to be considered. The category used at the time was *women*. This was used in opposition to the word *man*, which was considered universal and supposedly includes all human beings. Even today, in different everyday situations, many people talk or write about a group of people using the male form, even if the majority are women and even if only one man is present. This is what American feminists exposed of Freire, who used the masculine as universal. In Brazil, at the time of the Constituent Assembly in the 1980s, the term *gender* was not yet used. For this reason, in the Constitution of the Federative Republic of Brazil of 1988, the term *sex* was used. At that time, in the United States:

[what] people from the feminist movements were questioning was precisely that the universal, in our society, is masculine and that they did not feel included when they were named by the masculine. Thus, what the movement demanded was done in the name of 'Woman', not 'Man', showing that the 'universal man' did not include issues specific to 'woman'. As examples, we can mention the right to 'have children whenever you want, if you want' – the fight against domestic violence and the demand that household chores should be divided; in short, it was in the name of 'difference', in

relation to 'man' – here thought of as a universal, masculine being, that the category 'Woman' was claimed.

(Pedro 2005: 79–80)

Another issue was the need to refer to the movement as plural to better show its *waves* and connections with global political debates or society as a whole. Intellectuals of both sexes stimulated feminist movements. They prevailed because they found resonance among women from different social strata who gradually became aware of their social inferiority and the possibility of changing the reality to which they were subjected. According to Saffioti (1979: 160), quoting Lauretis: 'As a political–scientific perspective, feminism is born as a point of observation (or is confused with it) politically–ideologically committed to the denunciation of inequalities, asymmetries, domination, present in gender relations, and to the deconstruction–reconstruction of this reality and the concepts that do not apprehend it.'

Brazilian feminist movements had particular components from their own historical formation and dependence on hegemonic centres since the beginning of Brazilian colonization. In the Brazilian case, this historical formation process was characterized by the cultural marks of patriarchy, paternalism, conservatism and chauvinism.

Chauvinism refers to the excessive or prejudiced support for one's own cause or group, in particular male prejudice against women.

As elements to favour these aspects, the following deserve mention: 'slavery, the late emancipation of the center of domination, the influence of the Catholic Church as a political force and instrument of social control' (Toscano and Goldemberg 1992: 25). In Brazil, the first to take a stand was Nísia Floresta (1810–85), a precursor in the history of

Brazilian feminism. In 1920, Diva Nolf Nazario highlighted all the prejudices used as arguments to deny women's rights, such as the right to vote.

Both in Brazil and the rest of the world, women were excluded from the status of voters, even in countries where industrialization had already begun. This flag had only been raised by a few middle-class and bourgeois women with more advanced ideas, who had access to the international news and for whom this struggle demonstrated modernity and progress. According to Blay (cited by Augusta 1989: 9–19):

In the second half of the 18th century, the British Empire was consolidated, expanded, and industrialized. In all spheres of the English socio–economic world, there was a full sexual division, the role of women was strictly delimited and linked to the family [...] a great ideological frontier indicated the 'place' of women [...] the same French and English values were established here with the economic hegemony of those centers. In Rio Grande do Norte, a 22–year–old girl, Nísia Floresta, rebelled against the limitations imposed on women and sought, at the seat of economic and cultural power, the complicity of Mary Wollstonecraft [...] Nísia Floresta translates the book by Mary Vindication of The Rights of Women in free form.

Between the end of the Second Reign and the First World War, new ideas and doctrines arose, with the intensification of international relations, trips abroad, correspondence with foreign intellectuals from the higher and more educated classes, and the migratory flow from Europe to Brazil. The changes in this period also brought feminist ideas from Europe and demanded greater participation of women in political life and decision–making centres.

As an exponent of this struggle, in Brazil, Bertha Lutz, daughter of Adolfo Lutz, a renowned Brazilian doctor and scientist of Swiss origin, started an organized movement and became one of the first feminist leaders in the country.

Brazil went through a period of great political and social transformations between the two world wars. There was an intense exchange of ideas, controversies and discussions about the direction of Brazilian society, which was the scene of numerous events, such as the creation of the Brazilian Communist Party (1922), Tenentismo (1922–4), the Semana de Arte Moderna (1922), the Prestes Column (1924–7) and the Revolution of 1930, as well as the process of industrialization.

The growing presence of women in the world of work, their entry into schools of higher education, albeit in small numbers, and their participation in intellectual circles were evident. Still, there was resistance on the part of Congress regarding the female vote, even though feminists already had the support of many public men, deputies, senators and journalists (Brabo 2003). As Toscano and Goldemberg (1992: 27) point out, the speeches of congressmen against the recognition of women's right to vote 'were based on the thesis that the family would be threatened with extinction if this right were approved. [...] it was the paternalistic and authoritarian view of the legislators of the time'.

However, conservative reactions were not able to stop change. The influence of models imported from capitalist countries became increasingly present, affecting different levels of society, including the family. Thus, in 1932, the right to vote was approved, and in 1943, the labour legislation to protect women's work was implemented with the consolidation of labour laws. In this period, numerous associations, leagues and clubs were created to discuss women's participation and emancipation (Brabo 2003). These organizations did not defend contestation or structural changes in society. Still, they limited themselves to the conquest of new spaces in the world of work for women and the struggle for equality between the sexes.

From the 1960s onwards, the work of Simone de Beauvoir ([1949] 2009), *The Second Sex*, inspired a real renewal in feminist literature in Brazil, showing the advances and stagnations. After those feminist mobilizations, there was a growth in the theoretical production of the Brazilian female condition. In 1966, Rose Marie Muraro launched *A Mulher na Construção do Mundo Futuro*; in 1979, Professor Heleieth Saffioti, from Universidade Estadual Paulista, launched the book *Women in Class Society*; in 1974, the journalist Heloneida Stuart wrote the book *Woman, Object of Bed and Table*. Women's magazines also began to modify the content of their articles, emphasizing the need for women to question their role as housewives, encouraging the search for other forms of achievement, and keeping Brazilian paternalism and *machismo* in check (Brabo 2003).

In the 1970s, there was a turnaround in the feminist movement towards broader questions and a more critical stance, which later became the voice of militants and, in general, socialists. In 1972, with the National Council of Women of Brazil, led by Romy Medeiros da Fonseca, a lawyer from Rio de Janeiro, a congress was held in which representatives from various levels of society participated, alongside feminists with leftist positions, such as Rose Marie Muraro, Heleieth Saffioti and Carmen da Silva. From that congress onwards, the focus shifted to legal issues that affected women, which were later incorporated into the Civil Code, such as the principle of equality between husband and wife and the introduction of divorce into Brazilian legislation (Toscano and Goldemberg 1992).

In 1975, the International Year of Women, feminists started the Feminine Movement for Amnesty, mobilizing public opinion against the arbitrariness of the military government established with the 1964 coup in Brazil. In this period of extreme political repression, women took an effective position, rebelling against that policy and exercising their citizenship rights.

The media, books, TV, theatre and radio began to discuss women-related themes that had been forbidden until then. Thus, the discussion of women's rights and their inequality and inferiority in society reached many homes in different regions of the country, so the debate was not restricted to the elite. This gave a new impetus to the movement.

In this period in Brazil, one can assert that Freire has also contributed to the libertarian thinking of women, with the ideas systematized in the book *Education for Critical Consciousness*. In this book, according to Macedo and colleagues (2013), he makes a reflective review of his life trajectory and the choices and consequences of his decisions throughout his life. According to Macedo and colleagues, when the military forces took over the government, 'all progressive movements are suppressed, and Freire is accused of subversive activities, being arrested, on June 16, in the morning. [...] During this period of imprisonment he begins to write one of his first works, which he concludes in Chile – *Education for Critical Consciousness*' (2013: 35).

The authors also recall:

[W]hen asking for political asylum at the Bolivian embassy, he [Freire] could not remain there due to the coup that had taken place in that country. Due to the acquaintance with Ivan Illich, since 1962, when they met in Recife, he was invited to lecture and present conferences in Cuernavaca, Mexico. In 1966, Freire met Erich Fromm in that same city, who characterized Freire's educational practice as 'a kind of historical–sociocultural and political psychoanalyses.

(Freire cited in Macedo et al. 2013: 36)

Freire's international experience during his exile provided a new dimension for his work. In Chile, he had contact with unionists and workers, redefining his thesis, *Education for Critical Consciousness*, and expanding the critical reflection necessary to complete the work *Pedagogy of the Oppressed* (Macedo et al. 2013).

Paulo Freire: Meeting with American feminists

As we have already indicated, in the 1960s and 1970s, American feminism was in its *second wave*. Feminists expanded the debate about oppression and inequality, showing the subtler forms of the patriarchal system that contributed to maintaining gender inequality, including through language. At this time, North American feminists led Freire to critically reflect on the importance of language for reproducing stereotypes and the belief in man as a unique and universal model subject. Freire's encounter with feminists made him elaborate a critique of how the generic use of the masculine term – including 'man' – to refer to human beings constituted a way of strengthening and valuing the presence of men in the world and, at the same time, hiding the action of women, contributing to inequality.

Regarding the sexist language that predominated in his works, in a dialogue with Donaldo Macedo, Freire stated: 'I'm not apologizing for the sexist language in this book. I'm just clarifying that, during my formative years, I didn't escape the enveloping powers of a highly sexist culture in my country. However, I have tried to remove from my language all those characteristics that are degrading to women' (Freire, as cited in Macedo et al. 2013: 82).

In the book *Pedagogy of the Oppressed*, published in 1968, Freire refers to 'men in and with the world', with the conviction that the term *men* would encompass both men and women. He did not understand the sexist language implicit in his writings, which led to the criticisms mentioned above made by some American feminists. Also, as cited in Macedo and colleagues (2013: 259–60), Paulo Freire emphasized in 2001:

I believe that the question that feminists in the United States raise, which relates to my gender work in *Pedagogy of the Oppressed*, is not only valid but very accurate. Given the seriousness and complexity of the gender issue, this deserves reflection in conjunction with a rigorous analysis of the phenomenon of oppression. This also requires new pedagogical practices to achieve the dream of the struggle for liberation and victory over all forms of oppression. [...] It is with great satisfaction that I admit that my engagement with feminist movements has enabled me to focus more accurately on gender issues. For this, I am indebted to American feminists, who have drawn my attention on several occasions to gender discrimination. It was during the 1970s, after the publication of *Pedagogy of the Oppressed*, that I began to reflect more deeply and learn more systematically about the work of feminists.

Thus, the philosopher and educator recognized the sexist language that constitutes the *Pedagogy of the Oppressed*. Later, he reformulated his language, including the gender variable in his works. He not only recognized the sexist language present in his production but also undertook to revise the language in all his work, in addition to including the female gender in his discourse in other books, as can be seen in several of his works. For example, in *Pedagogy of Hope*, he writes: 'The dialogue between teachers and teachers and students does not make them equal, but it marks the democratic position between them' (Freire 1992: 60).

Final remarks

Freire's life story shows his permanent concern about freedom, social justice, revolutionary action and humanization, under the argument that all people should be provided the opportunity to *read the world*. According to Macedo and colleagues (2013), his identity 'from Recife, Pernambuco, Brazilian and Latin American is being built and, gradually, he is also becoming a world citizen, with an increasingly broader view of social issues'. His stay in the United States and other countries, his contact with workers and intellectuals and his experience in the World Council of Churches contributed to deepening and expanding his ideas, as expressed in his works.

Under the military coup, political persecution and exile, Freire had to adapt his life project and managed to extract lessons from each situation, including adversities, to learn from his own experience. When in exile, and based on his experiences in other contexts, he described himself as a *citizen of the world,* and he also influenced other scholars wherever he went, as Macedo and colleagues (2013) pointed out.

In the same way, feminist movements increasingly specified the various ways society naturalizes inequality, including what could be seen in terms of the use of language as referred to. As stated by Freire (1992: 36):

> It is not pure idealism [...] not to wait for the world to change radically to change the language. Changing language is part of the process of changing the world. The relationship between language–thought–world is a dialectical, procedural, contradictory relationship. It is clear that overcoming the sexist discourse, like overcoming any authoritarian discourse, demands, or places they need, concomitantly with the new, democratic, anti-discriminatory discourse, for us to engage in democratic practices as well. What is not possible is simply to make a democratic, anti-discriminatory discourse and have a colonial practice.

As we have discussed, this educator's ideas contributed to strengthening the action and struggle of all those subjected to social practices of oppression, including women. Freire believes education provides participatory citizen training, not training to be oppressed or dominated.

All the presuppositions of Freirean pedagogy remain up to date. They include learning to think autonomously, developing logical reasoning and working collaboratively, being the subject of knowledge, being open to new learning, understanding that knowledge is power, and elaborating on knowledge in a creative, challenging and provocative school. Today, amid so many scientific and technological advances, there is also a lack of humanity. This shows the timeliness of Freire's thought and the need to invest in human development at all levels of education and in all areas of knowledge as well as in the community, as he argues. Furthermore, it is necessary to educate oneself to select and critically review the avalanches of information transmitted by the numerous means of communication that sometimes replace human values, so dear to humanity and present in Freire's thought.

In the life and work of Paulo Freire, there is a deep passion for human freedom and, at the same time, a rigorous and constantly renewed search for an emancipatory pedagogy, in addition to the incessant search for coherence between discourse and practice. These values remain current and necessary for realizing a humane and just society.

References

Beauvoir, S. ([1949] 2009), *O Segundo Sexo*, trans. S. Milliet, Rio de Janeiro: Nova Fronteira.

Blay, E. A. (1989), 'Prefácio', in M. Wollstonecraft (ed), *Direitos das Mulheres e Injustiça dos Homens*, 4th edn, trans. N. F. B. Augusta, 9–15, São Paulo: Cortez.

Brabo, T. M. (2003), 'Género e Poder Local: Eleições Municipais em Marília (SP)', PhD diss., Faculdade de Filosofia, Letras e Ciências Humanas, Universidade de São Paulo, Brasil.

Brabo, T. M. (2005), *Cidadania da Mulher Professora*, São Paulo: Icone.

Brabo, T. M. (2008), *Gênero e Poder Local*, São Paulo: Humanitas, FAPESP.

Fougeyrollas-Schwebel, D. (2009), 'Movimentos Feministas', in H. Hirata, F. Laborie, H. Le Doaré and D. Senotier (eds), *Dicionário Crítico do Feminismo*, 144–5, São Paulo: UNESP.

Freire, P. ([1968] 1987), *Pedagogia do Oprimido*, 17th edn, Rio de Janeiro: Paz e Terra.

Freire, P. (1992), *Pedagogia da Esperança: Um Reencontro com a Pedagogia do Oprimido*, Rio de Janeiro: Paz e Terra.

Macedo, E., L. Vasconcelos, M. Evans, M. Lacerda and M. Vaz Pinto (2013), *Revisitando Paulo Freire: Sentidos na Educação*, Brasília: Liber Livro.

Muraro, R. M. (1966a), *A Mulher na Construção do Mundo Futuro*, Petrópolis: Vozes.

Pedro, J. M. (2005), 'Traduzindo o Debate: o Uso da Categoria Gênero na Pesquisa Histórica', *História*, 24 (1): 77–98.

Pinto, C. J. (2003), *Uma História do Feminismo no Brasil*, São Paulo: Fundação Perseu Abramo.

Saffioti, H. B. (1979), *A Mulher na Sociedade de Classes: Mito e Realidade*, Petrópolis: Vozes.

Studart, H. (1974), *Mulher: Objeto de Cama e Mesa*, Petrópolis: Vozes.

Toscano, M. and M. Goldemberg (1992), *A Revolução das Mulheres: Balanço do Feminismo no Brasil*, Rio de Janeiro: Revan.

PART TWO

Pedagogy, Education, Body and Sexualities

CHAPTER THREE

A Second Chance in School: A Look at *Precious* through Freire

*María José Chisvert-Tarazona
and Pilar Cambronero-García*

Introduction

This chapter explores Freire's influence and that of popular education within the cinematic story *Precious* (2009). This film shows the pedagogical relationship between a teenager and a teacher and the transformation process of the main character, Precious, born out of mutual respect and equal dialogue. Cinematic language is an instrument of communication, collective education and a cultural repository that brings us closer to representations of reality through artistic and documentary narratives (Chisvert-Tarazona 2013). In Clarembeaux's (2010) words, cinema is the art of collective and individual memory.

The objective of this chapter is to analyse how Precious uses the small space of freedom granted to her in this unique school, how she learns to listen to her voice, to claim her right to education and a decent life.

Technical specifications of the film

Precious (2009) is an adaptation of *Push*, Ramona Lofton's first novel (Table 1). It tells the story of Clareece 'Precious' Jones, a poor, obese, illiterate Black teenager. This intersectionality (Brah and Phoenix 2004) of social status, body shape, culture and age makes her a victim of the most demeaning abuses. In the film, director Lee Daniels offers a closer look at the main character's life project from an educational perspective.

The story and its relationship with Freire's school of thought

The main character, Clareece Precious, lives in Harlem. The absence of freedom, humiliation and degradation characterizes her existence. Precious is forced to have sexual intercourse with her father, obey a mother who constantly disparages her and eventually drop out of school because of her pregnancy. Freire ([1968] 1975) would refer to this as objectification and dehumanization. It seems there is no way out for Precious until she is offered the opportunity to attend an alternative educational institution: a literacy centre that follows an educational system called *Each One/Teach One*,[1] where, in addition to learning, the students actively participate in the teaching process. At this moment, Freire's school of thought becomes apparent. The film recreates the human dimension of education as a practice of freedom (Freire [1968] 1975), which in a regime of domination can only be produced and developed from a pedagogy of the oppressed. That is a humanistic and liberating pedagogy in which the oppressed reveal the world of oppression and commit themselves, in praxis, to its transformation.

TABLE 1 Technical specifications of *Precious* (2009)

Original title: Precious (based on the novel *Push* by Sapphire)
Year: 2009
Running time: 105 min.
Country: United States
Director: Lee Daniels
Screenwriter: Geoffrey Fletcher (Novel: Sapphire)
Cinematography: Andrew Dunn
Cast: Gabourey Sidibe, Mo'Nique, Paula Patton, Mariah Carey, Sherri Shepherd, Lenny Kravitz
Producer: Lee Daniels Entertainment/Smokewood Entertainment Group
Genre: Drama
Synopsis: Clareece 'Precious' Jones (Gabourey Sidibe) is an obese, Black teenager from Harlem who is constantly abused physically and emotionally by her mother (Mo'Nique). She does not know how to read or write and is expelled from school when they discover that she is pregnant. In spite of everything, the director of the center enrols her in an alternative school so that she can try to redirect her life. Her new teacher (Paula Patton) is the first person Precious trusts and who treats her with respect.
Awards in 2009:
  Two Academy Awards: Best Adapted Screenplay, Supporting Actress (Mo'Nique). Six nominations.
  Golden Globes: Best Supporting Actress (Mo'Nique). Three nominations.
  BAFTA Awards: Best Sup. Actress (Mo'Nique). Four nominations, including Best Film.
  Sundance Film Festival: Grand Jury Prize, Audience Award.
  Toronto Film Festival: Best Movie (Audience Award).
  Five Independent Spirit Awards: including Best Film, Director and Actress (Sidibe).
  Los Angeles Film Critics Association: Best Supp. Actress (Mo'Nique).
  American Film Institute (AFI): Top 10 – Movies of the Year.
  Critics' Choice Awards: Best Supporting Actress (Mo'Nique). Six nominations.

Source: FilmAffinity.

> In a Freirean view, **praxis** reports to the strong marriage between reflection (theory) and action, which need to work together to promote change in the world.

In the first lesson, Ms Rain, the teacher, asks Clareece to sit in the front row. Next, she invites the girls to share something about themselves. The film sequence is very intense and ends with Clareece becoming aware of her voice, of expressing who she is, what she likes, what she knows what to do and how she feels in a public space:

Ms Rain: Something you do well?
Clareece: Nothing.
Ms Rain: Everyone is good at something.
Clareece: Well, I can cook… and I've never spoken in class before.
Ms Rain: How does it make you feel?
Clareece: Here. It makes me feel like I'm here.

> **E**mpowerment is a process through which people gain power and control over their lives. This implies that they are provided by their communities with the support they need to become citizens who enjoy equal rights, including recognition.

This is when her empowerment in the real world begins, not only in her fantasy world. A transition takes place from dehumanization to humanization, where the oppressed restore their freedom without damaging the freedom of the oppressor (Freire [1968] 1975). Ms Rain teaches Clareece how to read and write. She encourages her to keep a journal and participate in class. Popular knowledge and scientific knowledge become connected through the experiences of the world (Freire [1981] 1992).

In this school, acquiring literacy means learning to write and witness your life narrative through your own story. For Clareece, reading and writing become an opportunity to 'be'. Ms Rain introduces her students to a pedagogy they can take ownership of. The paths of freedom are those of the oppressed who free themselves: Clareece is not someone who is rescued but a woman who reconfigures herself responsibly, takes charge of her life, takes on the upbringing of her children, and continues to learn and teach.

The Pedagogy of the Oppressed liberates Clareece, the oppressed, and her mother, the oppressor, as it allows them to move towards a liberating reality. In line with Hegel, we would say that the truth of the one who oppresses resides in the conscience of the one who is oppressed. In one of the film's last scenes, the social worker brings mother and daughter together. For the first time, the oppressor's reasons are made explicit in a dialogue, almost a monologue, that makes her aware of her mistake.

This literacy process promotes a humanistic pedagogy: the person who learns, recognizes and represents him/herself through personal action, a process in which consciousness is not only knowledge or recognition but option, decision, commitment and action. Teaching and learning require the conviction that 'changing the world is as difficult as possible' (Freire 2000: 39).

In this film, the exercise of individual freedom is evidenced through female characters. Clareece's empowerment is centred on education, a desire mediated by the process of liberation.

Conscientization: The move from object to subject

Objectification of Clareece is linked to the different social scenarios that surround it. It is not a natural characteristic of any social group or individual. Objectification is the result of social regulation; it is a construct. It responds to the dominant ideas of each context and historical period, which are connected to the social interests of the organized structures of the social control systems. Without a doubt, Clareece is not considered a subject because of the intersectionality of certain parameters of objectification constructed in the West: she is a Black African American, obese, young and poor female.

People's actions depend on the surrounding place, time, and situations, activities and attributes that are praised, condemned or ignored. Karsz (2000) alludes to social vulnerability as a prelude to exclusion.

Freire ([1968] 1975) argues that the absence of individual freedom, such as that experienced by the film's protagonist, places one in a space of oppression. He defends the reflective awareness of one's historical constraints as a path to liberation. His confidence in the ability of education to transform the world through individual freedom as a member of a social group leads us to analyse the limits of institutionalized educational interaction. Educators need to step down from their pedestal of moral authority, as implied by *banking education*, and socialize with the students, as Freire's liberating pedagogy implies. That is what Ms Rain does. She takes sides, gets involved, generates a bond and humanizes the pedagogical relationship.

The critical–dialogical pedagogy in the film

In the schools of the agrarian farms occupied by the Brazilian Landless Worker's Movement, one can read: 'We believe in a school that awakens the dreams of our youth, that cultivates solidarity, hope and the desire to learn, teach and transform the world.' These words simplify and summarize the principles that sustain critical pedagogy, an emancipatory tradition that shelters the work of Freire: (1) education is not neutral; (2) society can be transformed through the commitment of conscious and critical people; and (3) praxis connects social transformation with liberating education (Boyce 1996).

This transformative pedagogical philosophy invites learners to re-evaluate their social order in search of greater gender, racial and economic justice (McLaren 1997).

> **C**ritical pedagogy stands on a transformative pedagogical philosophy that argues for the need to know the world to be able to transform it. Learning to read the world is led by the need to understand it to promote its change.

Freire ([1968] 1975) deeply disagreed with the dominant *banking education*. This term referred to the use of education as an instrument of oppression in opposition to popular education. *Banking education* can be defined as an oppressive instrument that sees the learner as a passive and ignorant subject who must learn by memorizing and repeating the contents. Oppositely, in *liberating popular education*, learning does not coincide with the teacher's knowledge but is the result of the dialogue between the experience and knowledge of educators and students. It is a matter of revealing different knowledge and experiences that are inherently different and enabling learning that is shared, critical, of cultural creation, and not of transmission. Clareece entered an alternative school after going through a formal education that did not want to abandon her but did not know how to help her.

It is important to be aware of how school culture tends to legitimize inequality. Those who fail in the educational system internalize their inferiority or must admit that they have not tried hard enough. That is how Clareece expressed it in the film: 'They kicked me out because I was pregnant.' In this way, the educational system is exempt from all responsibility. The ideology of effort is not innocent.

As Freire proposed, in line with critical pedagogy, transformative education approaches a common intellectual, moral and action approach, which can be described as critical, emancipatory and transformative. Ms Rain respects Clareece and her learning pace; she teaches her to read, think and make decisions.

Analysis regarding critical pedagogy carried out from the neoliberal conservative field is added to those led by postmodernity, questioning its foundations. In line with deconstruction, relativism supports the 'critique of criticism', the destruction of metanarratives and the criticism of new Foucauldian regimes of truth. Sordé, Flecha and Godás (1998) condemn how postmodern philosophy contributes to deactivating opposition movements. It arouses mistrust about the transformative possibilities and reduces the generation of proposals encouraging change.

According to Jean François Lyotard, **metanarratives** are grand narratives that try to give comprehensive accounts of historical experiences, events, and social and cultural processes, appealing to universal truth and values. Traditionally, religion, family and the State are examples of these.

However, a second modernity is making its way, fuelled by social movements that recognize egalitarian dialogue as a place from which to transform the world as differences become cherished. This egalitarian dialogue can be observed in Clareece's diary and her epistolary relationship with Ms Rain when Clareece is in the hospital: 'Dear Precious, your main responsibility is with yourself. [...] Where was your grandmother when your father abused you? Where is little Mongo? What is best for you in this situation?' Her questions and reflections force Clareece to delve into her situation and emotions as oppression limit situations (Freire [1968] 1975) that must be dealt with. She answers: 'You ask too many questions. Sometimes I wish I could stop breathing. I just want to be a good mother.'

Freire's contributions to a liberating *pedagogy of hope* are alive in the film. The school (i) values egalitarian dialogue while considering that the entire community builds reality and knowledge; (ii) is committed to the transformation of the learning environment rather than shaping the student; and (iii) proposes the equality of differences instead of diversity. What is at stake here is the right to experience one's options in the face of homogenization.

Dialogical feminism in educational code

Freire, Habermas and Beck are some of the most significant authors of what has been called second modernity (Beck [1986] 2006). Dialogue becomes a key element for the fluid coexistence of a diverse society.

Thus, in the same vein, dialogical feminism includes the voices of all women, establishing the principle of equality of differences. It seeks to 'defend a radicalization of democratic processes to jointly elaborate a theory that allows a single definition of femininity' (Beck-Gernsheim, Butler and Puigvert 2001: 52). It is an inclusive definition that does not homogenize women but supports them to become an active part of the movement, making their voice audible and their diverse identities visible.

Entering the scene of culture implies creating spaces where the voice of the dialoguing subject referred to by Freire ([1981] 1992) can be heard, opening the door to a collective knowledge acquired through individual freedom and aimed at making the collective voice for liberation. However, feminism, and our main character, has a specific nature that seeks to recover desire, communication and thinking, an assertive posture that favours women's capacity for self-assertion and historical action.

In this process, the infinite possibilities of life in each relationship are shown, creating new meanings that destabilize patriarchal networks and establish new forms of relationship with the social and the symbolic. In the same way, in the 'pedagogy of the oppressed', the confrontation of opposites is recognized as necessary, that is, the struggle, the conflict of the oppressed to liberate themselves from the oppressors.

In the film, Clareece experiences new relationships with the world by venturing beyond the assigned places of gender and other locations of oppression and arrives at the edge, where the danger lies. Precious's desire to return to the last row in class is not reason enough to stop; it is sustained by the 'world–word' (Freire [1981] 1992). Freire points out that reading the world precedes reading the word; language and reality are dynamically connected, and the critical reading of written texts implies the perception of the relationships between text and context.

Because empowerment is dynamic, it is a process of change aimed at a complex adaptation to the environment. Motivation is key, but the presence of women is not enough; it also requires having the appropriate means for development and access to the necessary resources. That is why the work carried out in the school is so relevant.

Intertwined with the narrative of empowerment is the narrative of constant oppression. Despite the main character's determination, she alone cannot escape a system that contributes to her oppression, a system with minimal opportunities where the weight of patriarchy and capitalism are strongly present.

Freire ([1981] 1992) invites education professionals to be consistent with his discourse: commitment and hope. The 'other women' who live on the edge, outside the public space, at risk of vulnerability, show their ability to transform reality (Freire 1997) day by day through popular universities and literacy classes and with their struggle.

Final remarks

A popular feminist education allows women to teach and learn together, critically analysing their lives, contexts and the most important issues, allowing them to move from vulnerability and oppression, as conceptualized by Freire, to empowerment. The literacy space shown in *Precious* (2009) is a good example of this ideological positioning of liberation, an educational practice that seeks to create a safe space of trust and solidarity where different voices can emerge.

The school is aware of the context and seeks to promote learning through actions related to specific problems and practical solutions.

As this film illustrates, the key to transformation lies in prioritizing reflection, dialogue and action as the main path to learning. This attitude requires an exercise of visibility that allows diversity, power dynamics and conflict to be addressed. Recovering popular knowledge, popular culture (Freire [1981] 1992) and women's daily experiences, together with using history, art, theatre and other artistic forms, generates open questions that promote critical and creative analysis, deepening the understanding of power.

Making this change requires encouraging women's sense of hope, inspiration, and joy to be expressed and introducing time for self-care and personal renewal.

It is relevant to reinterpret knowledge, learn to think, do, use knowledge independently and relate it to one's life.

Following Giroux (1990), knowledge is not studied in emancipatory education but is presented as a mediation between the individual and the broader social reality. In the same line, Freire ([1968] 1975) asserts that we learn with one another mediated by the world.

Education is not purely a matter of cognitive instruments but is built through relationships between people. It is not about applying external 'techniques' to one's existence but about an experiential experience that creates freedom (Freire [1981] 1992). It is a search that seduces our heroine and all those who venture in the direction of finding themselves. This brief film analysis shows that creating conditions for this is also the role of society and its institutions, not just an individual endeavour.

Note

1   During the period of slavery in the United States, when African people were denied education, including learning how to read, a pedagogical strategy of great transformative power was devised: when an enslaved person learned how to read, this person must teach someone else, which generated the phrase '*Each One/ Teach One*'.

References

Beck, U. ([1986] 2006), *La Sociedad del Riesgo: Hacia una Nueva Modernidad*, Barcelona: Paidós.

Beck-Gernsheim, E., J. Butler and L. Puigvert (2001), *Mujeres y Transformaciones Sociales*, Esplugues de Llobregat: El Roure.

Boyce, M. (1996), 'Organizational Story and Storytelling: A Critical Review', *Journal of Organizational Change Management*, 9 (5): 5–26.

Brah, A. and A. Phoenix (2004), 'Ain't I a Woman? Revisiting Intersectionality', *Journal of International Women Studies*, 5 (3): 75–86.

Chisvert-Tarazona, M. J. (2013), 'La Responsabilidad Social de las Universidades a Través de la Memoria Cinematográfica', *Revista de Docencia Universitaria. REDU*, 11 (1): 389–410.

Clarembeaux, M. (2010), 'Educación en Cine: Memoria y Patrimonio', *Comunicar*, 35 (XVIII): 25–32.

Freire, P. ([1968] 1975), *Pedagogia do Oprimido*, Porto: Afrontamento.

Freire, P. ([1981] 1992), *A Importância do Ato de Ler: Em Três Artigos que se Completam*, São Paulo: Cortez.

Freire, P. (1997), *Pedagogía de la Autonomía: Saberes Necesarios para la Práctica Educativa*, Buenos Aires: Siglo XXI.

Freire, P. (2000), *Pedagogia da Indignação: Cartas Pedagógicas e Outros Escritos*, São Paulo: UNESP (FEU).

Giroux, H. A. (1990), *Los Profesores como Intelectuales: Hacia una Pedagogía Critica del Aprendizaje*, Barcelona: Paidós.

Karsz, S. (2000), *L'exclusion, Définir pour en Finir*, Paris: Dunod.

McLaren, P. (1997), *Pedagogía Crítica y Cultura Depredadora*, Barcelona: Paidós.

Precious (2009), [Film] Dir. Lee Daniels, US: Lee Daniels Entertainment, Smokewood Entertainment Group.

Sordé, T., R. Flecha and X. Godás (1998), 'Postmodernisme i moviments socials', *Revista Catalana de Sociología*, (7): 135–58.

CHAPTER FOUR

Sex Education: An *Untested Feasibility* for Homosexual Young People in School

Sofia Almeida Santos

CIIE – Centre for Research and Intervention in Education of the Faculty of Psychology and Education Sciences, University of Porto, Portugal[1]

This chapter focuses on the possibilities and limits of school sex education for addressing the rights of homosexual sexual–affective diversity. It analyses how the *school ethos* and practices offer resistance conditions and provides impulses to discuss new *relational ethics* within the framework of sexual and intimate citizenship. The relevance of sexuality in the social culture of contemporary youth, together with the emergence of new sexual claims, makes it pertinent to reaffirm the place of education in the public agenda of sexual rights. To this end, the dialogue between Paulo Freire's and *feminist thought* acquires centrality to understanding, on the one hand, (in)visible forms of oppression that persist in schools, and on the other, how the educational experience leads to a new awareness of self, 'as a new sense of dignity that is stirred by a new hope' (Freire [1968] 2005: 33). Moreover, Freirean reflections allow an understanding of how sexual–affective discrimination and invisibility may emerge as limit situations of oppression in young people's construction as authors of their own story. This question is crucial and deserves attention. In this brief reflection, I bring to the fore some perceptions of teachers and young people on the challenges of being homosexual at school, a situation often experienced as a 'limiting situation of oppression' that many of us continue to ignore, and that school sex education might be transformed into an 'untested feasibility' by providing opportunities for conscientization and change, within the school environment and beyond.

According to Freire, a **limit situation** refers to the constraints that oppress groups and individuals. If they limit the experience of being human by turning people into objects, they also open the grounds for change by means of conscientization, a concept we delved into above.

What is at stake here?

In recent decades, diversity, equality and inclusion issues have gained social and political relevance in Portugal. In this regard, it is worth recalling some recent legal landmarks regarding sexual and gender rights: the decriminalization of voluntary interruption of pregnancy by women (up to the first ten weeks) in 2007 (Law no. 16/2007); the same-sex marriage law in 2010 (Law no. 9/2010); or the first gender identity law in 2011 (Law no. 7/2011), subsequently upgraded in 2018 by the legal gender recognition on self-determination to include the possibility to change legal gender at the age of sixteen, depending on parental consent and a doctor's report.

Fuelled by these legislative advances, the educational sector has also made acknowledged progress in this field. The bill on school-based sex education that, for the first time, includes sexual diversity and gender identity in the curriculum (Law no. 60/2009) or the recent introduction of compulsory citizenship education (Law no. 55/2018) came as evidence of that drift. There has been a clear shift of political action towards citizenship rights, making Portugal one of the most egalitarian countries in Europe in terms of lesbian, gay, bisexual, transgender and intersex (LGBTI) individuals' legal rights. That is why it remains surprising that there is still a lack of specific policies and plans to protect LGBTI students at schools.

According to the 2022 report on the experiences of homosexual youth in Portuguese schools, most participants reported experiences of discrimination and homophobic bullying, as well as underrepresentation in the curriculum. Schools remain featured as 'hostile environments', where LGBT students choose to be 'invisible' (Fernandes, Alves and Gato 2022). As a result, the negative impact of these experiences in terms of mental health, well-being and educational success is professionals' responsibility. From the moment that schools do not seem to keep up with current challenges and the access to education is mitigated based on sexual orientation, this issue becomes urgent.

This clash between policy and practice highlights how the understanding of the 'good' sexual citizen contrasts with the processes of marginalization and oppression still experienced by some sexual and gender groups in schools. This is due, in part, to cultural resistance to implementing the education of sexuality as a public right and duty. Indeed, throughout history, education about sexuality at schools has always emerged as a political, controversial and contested issue. 'It invokes party political conflicts over policy' (Alldred and David 2007), dealing with a set of forces, particular meanings and power relations (Santos 2015; Santos and Macedo 2020). These tensions are evident in the Portuguese case, as a southern European Catholic country that struggles with being a young democracy (fifty years old) trying to rise to the social and educational demands posed by its European Union membership and global change.

Within this discussion, Paulo Freire's contributions, allied to feminist thought, bring interesting insights into the thinking of sex education as a practice of liberation through self- and collective awareness, inclusion and rupture with the situations of oppression, in and out of schools. The liberating educational approach is a condition for exercising sexual citizenship, bringing hope that those who do not fit into normative *compulsive heterosexuality* are not kicked to the curb. As the author states:

> There is no such thing as a *neutral* educational process. Education either functions as an instrument that is used to facilitate the integration of the younger generation into the logic of the present system and bring about conformity to it, *or* it becomes 'the practice of freedom', how men and women deal critically and creatively with reality and discover how to participate in the transformation of their world.
>
> (Freire [1968] 2005: 34)

Next, the potential of school sex education as a key context to learn sexual diversity as a right of citizenship is discussed based on a set of students' and teachers' perceptions of how homosexual diversity is (1) addressed in the curriculum and (2) experienced at school.

Educational dialogues with sexual–affective diversity

Sexual and intimate citizenship debates are important in recognizing sexual–affective diversity, as well as school-based sex education itself as a human right (Santos 2018). The concept of sexual citizenship (Richardson and Turner 2001), commonly seen as a paradox (Weeks 2010), brought inalienable sexual rights into the public arena, confronting a long history of hegemonic sexual politics. Following feminist and later LGBT criticism of essentialist categories such as compulsory heterosexuality and hegemonic masculinity, the first claim was for equal rights among sexual groups. By becoming 'politicized identities' (Richardson and Monro 2012), feminists, gays and lesbians required new *relational ethics*. This means that to be fully achieved, sexual recognition, self-awareness, consent and pleasure imply a 'democratic restructuring of intimate relations' where people choose what they do with their bodies, feelings, identities and relationships (Plummer 2003). Therefore, transforming interpersonal relationships (Giddens 1992) implies a new politics of daily life (Plummer 2003) and vice versa. Within this agenda of sexual rights, a rights-based approach to sex education emerges as the only guarantee that all children and young people can learn about their rights regarding gender, sexual, intimate, affective and reproductive decisions. Sex education is then a public right to access information and exercise citizenship.

This discussion informs how homosexual young people continue to live in schools.

This reflection is grounded in a mixed-methods approach, utilizing data from eighteen individual interviews with students – ten girls and eight boys aged sixteen to eighteen from a range of schools, from urban centres to more peripheral areas in Portugal. It also includes insights from ten interviews with key educational stakeholders – two male and eight female teachers across various disciplines including Citizenship Education, Science, Moral Education and Sports. Additional perspectives were gathered from tutors, psychologists, school nurses and head teachers, enriching the understanding of the educational landscape.

Two questions were asked to students and teachers: Has sex education ever addressed issues of sexual diversity? And what is it like to be homosexual at school? Their viewpoints are presented below.

(1) Left out of sex education curriculum: invisible oppression

We never talked **about it.** No one speaks about **those things.** (Female, 16)

The school never covered that. Never! It's an **untouchable issue.** (Male, 16)

Not a big topic. It was just the basics. They just said, treat your partner right. (Male, 15)

I've never received education **on that.** (Female, 16)

Students' reactions to the question of getting information and knowledge on sexual diversity reveal the persistent omission, absence and ignorance surrounding it. There is a common difficulty in even mentioning terms related to LGBT groups, opting to replace them with 'those things' or 'that'. Apparently, schools are still shrouded in an official silence that feeds the idea of non-existence and non-entitlement of some people. The invisibility to which some sexual identities are relegated in the syllabus and school discourse reinforces power relations of oppression (domination/subordination) since knowledge that fails to be included in the curriculum is de-legitimized and socially devalued. As mentioned, educational policies must be understood in broader political and cultural interests. The education of sexual rights is not learned and taught in a *vacuum,* but how it is taught and what is taught conveys specific norms and patterns of a society. As Allen (2011: 44) pointed out, education is not simply a 'neutral assemblage of knowledge [...] [but rather a] selective tradition, someone's selection, some group's vision of legitimate knowledge'. Therefore, its selection 'reflects both the distribution of power and the principles of social control' (Bernstein 1971: 47). So, we need to be aware of what is left out of the curriculum to analyse how sexual culture is built. The following excerpts demonstrate how the absence of representation leads to isolation, oppression and the exclusion of all those who do not fit into what, in 1990, Butler called the *heterosexual matrix*.

> We should definitely **be taught about** that because I've got friends whom I went to school with who are gay, and **they weren't ever told that was okay.** They were just told, 'this is how you have sex'. (Female, 17)

> We've been taught just about sex between men and women… **We haven't talked about any other sexualities at all,** and when they mentioned coming to puberty, it was **'boys you'll be attracted to girls and girls you'll be attracted to boys'.** Just about heterosexual relationships… I think they should, at least, **mention homosexuals… because they are in school.** They will be there, and they might not get the sex education everybody else does because it's just not mentioned. (Female, 17)

Heteronormalizing spaces are places where only heterosexuals are recognized (defined as 'normal'). All people are supposed to fit into that norm and behave as so.

The lack of recognition of homosexual young people defines schools as 'heteronormalizing spaces' and sex education as 'heteronormative practices' (Allen 2011: 3): spaces and practices where heterosexuals constitute the dominant group as subjects, and all others are constituted in subordination as dehumanized objects (Freire [1968] 2005). This separation between (the valued) 'us' and (the unvalued) 'them' 'denies lesbian, gay, and bisexual young people a legitimated social space and language for reflecting upon a defining part of their personal and social identity' (Baker, Lynch, Cantillon and Walsh 2004: 155).

Therefore, these perceptions of students feature schools as shapers of 'normative heterosexual identities' (Epstein, O'Flynn and Telford 2003: 10), reproducing gender and sexual stereotypes and inequalities (Louro 2000; Nayak and Kehily 2008). With the awareness that what is left out 'can be more powerful than what is spoken' (Thomson and Scott 1992: 13), the promotion of sexual citizenship rights is thus being denied to those who are absent from the curriculum, which hinders the development of democratic, equal relations and perpetuates situations of oppression.

(2) Homophobia: visible oppression

School is not prepared to deal with it. There are many prejudices. (Female, 15)

If the absence of content related to sexual diversity consigns homosexual students to invisibility and dehumanization, the inability of others to accept and include them puts these same students in the spotlight. The way people dress, talk, walk and flirt is scrutinized in corridors, classrooms and changing rooms. Bodies and emotions cannot be hidden. That is why the emergence of sexual diversity at schools is still turbulent, despite political pressures to tackle homophobic violence. Most students refer to this question based on friends' experiences who faced 'horrible', embarrassing situations. The comments and insults such as 'butch', 'faggot' or 'gay' are part of daily life at school.

People are still not very open about it. I've got an experience… a friend of mine is bisexual, and some people take advantage of that. **They never accept the fact that he is gay. I think they are cruel.** […] teachers just ignore it; they don't have to deal with it… (Male, 15)

If you are having those feelings, it must be a horrible situation… I don't think that education accommodates those kinds of people, definitely not. **My gay friend was subjected to horrible comments.** (Female, 17)

It's wrong to be homosexual. [...] I'm against it. The world was made with a purpose; now, many people are trying to change it. [...] I can be a friend of a gay since they don't mess or flirt with me. (Male, 15)

Including gay people is 'mitigated' and looked upon with 'strangeness' (Fonseca and Santos 2015). People learn the dynamics of oppression in it. For instance, the following excerpt shows how the oppressors are also oppressed.

When we see a person who looks homosexual by how s/he dresses, walks, or talks... if we are in a group, we immediately tend to make fun of them, but if we are alone, we look at the situation as if it is normal... (Male, 15)

This is a clear example of how inter- and intra-gender policing pushes youngsters towards dichotomous and hegemonic conceptions of sexuality that hinder sexual citizenship achievement.

Additionally, some teachers also highlighted homophobia among students as the greatest prejudice at schools.

The worst and the most prejudiced at school is homophobia. Massively strong. It is shocking. It is not taken seriously [by staff]. **It still hasn't engrained itself in the culture of the teaching staff. It's an institutional prejudice.** (Male teacher)

I see homosexuality with the greatest indifference, but the kids reject homosexuality. **It's very difficult to come out in schools.** (Female teacher)

They also refer to it with apparent indifference as if they were not an integral and central part of the 'institutional prejudice'. As mentioned, learning practices are not neutral;

instead, they are determined by 'the identity of the teacher, the hierarchal structure of the school and the teaching process' (Kehily 2002: 2). Therefore, teachers' awareness of sexual rights and the way they see their capacity to create moments that enhance students' awareness as oppressors/oppressed is fundamental. The absence of this self-concept as educators reinforces teachers' disengagement from supporting students' learning on this issue, choosing not to address it and increasing the non-recognition of some sexual groups.

> I'm very limited in it, but this school is tolerant [among students]. (Male teacher)

> I do not understand homosexuality much. It pains me a lot to watch them physically together. [...] There was a girl who wanted to become transexual. It was horrible. We didn't know what to do with her or how to proceed. Sometimes, I said, 'You look so beautiful today,' so she didn't feel excluded. (Female teacher)

We can notice that homosexuality enters the school through homophobia and not from sexual rights, placing homosexuals in limit-situations of oppression informed by their affective–sexual diversity.

Sex education: An *untested feasibility* in education

Based on these testimonies, on the one hand, the ignorance and conflict in which young people grow up concerning their sexual–affective rights can be identified, and on the other, some lethargy of teachers regarding their practice to change. Schools continue to reproduce a 'culture of silence' of the dispossessed. Rather than being encouraged and equipped to respond to the reality in which they are submerged, people continue to learn to be within trajectories of oppression. Freire ([1968] 2005: 32) enlightened this discussion, stressing that although the whole educational system remains one of the major instruments for the maintenance of this culture of silence, 'every human being, no matter how "ignorant" or submerged in the "culture of silence" he or she may be in, is capable of looking critically at the world in a dialogical encounter with others'. Within this context, sex education is key to providing such encounters by giving the proper tools so that everybody has the opportunity to become conscious of their perception of reality and deal critically with it in their relationship with others and mediated by the world. This means that students and teachers might perceive social and personal reality and its contradictions to transform the situation of oppression as the ultimate objective of conscientization. As seen, most youngsters feel oppressed and afraid of dialogue with their peers in their role as sexual–affective oppressors because those youngsters have been introjected and many times reproduced the myths that the oppressors use to legitimate their dominant sexual position. Hence, through sex education, oppressed homosexual young people may find room to acquire a critical awareness of their oppression, confront their reality and act upon it. This may include the liberation of the oppressors *if* and *when* they become aware of their role in embracing a world where sexual–affective diversity is delegitimized and valued.

A friend of mine suffers from that [pressure]. A lot. Because they suspected he was homosexual. They did many things to him. In the dressing room, the boys did not undress until he left. They mistreated him and insulted him, which had consequences later. He started to self-mutilate, dropped out of school, did not eat and his grades… Suddenly, one day, he was in the classroom and rebelled. He stood up and reported everything they had done to him. He dared to assume and face them. After that, they stopped teasing him. Teachers usually don't know these things. Nothing ever happens inside the classroom; outside is where it all happens. (Male, 15)

This testimony reveals a situation of mutual liberation as key in the process of acceptance, understanding and inclusion. The student looked critically at the social situation in which he found himself and confronted it critically. A new awareness of selfhood led him to surmount the *limiting situation*. He felt entitled as a sexual citizen to transform his situation but also that of his peers. A mere perception of reality would not lead to it. That is why education, and in this case, sex education, is an indispensable condition for accomplishing sexual citizenship rights using the resolution of sexual–affective limiting situations of oppression in young people's lives.

Note

1   Acknowledgements: This work is also supported by the Portuguese government, through the Foundation for Science and Technology, IP (FCT), under the multi-year funding awarded to CIIE (grants no. UIDB/00167/2020 and UIDP/00167/2020).

References

Alldred, P. and M. David (2007), *Get Real about Sex: The Politics and Practices of Sex Education*, Berkshire: McGraw-Hill, Open University Press.

Allen, L. (2011), *Young People and Sexuality Education: Rethinking Key Debates*, London: Palgrave Macmillan.

Baker, J., K. Lynch, S. Cantillon and J. Walsh (2004), *Equality: From Theory to Action*, New York: Palgrave Macmillan.

Bernstein, B. (1971), 'On the Classification and Framing of Educational Knowledge', in M. Young (ed), *Knowledge and Control: New Directions for the Sociology of Education*, 47–69, London: Collier MacMillan.

Butler, J. (1990), *Gender Trouble: Feminism and the Subversion of Identity*, New York: Routledge.

Epstein, D., S. O'Flynn and D. Telford (2003), *Silenced Sexualities in Schools and Universities*, Sterling, IL: Trentham Books.

Fernandes, T., B. Alves and J. Gato (2022), 'The FREE Project: Relatório preliminar sobre jovens LGBTQ+ e clima escolar em Portugal', *ZENODO*, 17 May. Available online: https://doi.org/10.5281/zenodo.6553126.

Fonseca, L. and S. A. Santos, eds (2015), *Sexualidades, Gravidez e Juventude: Relações Sociais e Educativas*, Porto: Afrontamento.

Freire, P. ([1968] 2005), *Pedagogy of the Oppressed*, New York: Continuum.

Giddens, A. (1992), *The Transformation of Intimacy: Sexuality, Love & Eroticism in Modern Societies*, Cambridge: Polity Press.

Kehily, M. J. (2002), *Sexuality, Gender and Schooling: Shifting Agendas in Social Learning*, London: Routledge Falmer.

Louro, G. (2000), *Currículo, Género e Sexualidade*, Porto: Porto Editora.

Nayak, A. and M. J. Kehily (2008), *Gender, Youth and Culture: Young Masculinities and Femininities*, New York: Palgrave Macmillan.

Plummer, K. (2003), *Intimate Citizenship: Private Decisions and Public Dialogues*, Seattle, WA, and London: University of Washington Press.

Richardson, D. and S. Monro (2012), *Sexuality, Equality & Diversity*, New York: Palgrave Macmillan.

Richardson, E. and B. Turner (2001), 'Sexual, Intimate or Reproductive Citizenship?', *Citizenship Studies*, 5 (3): 329–38.

Santos, S. A. (2015), *School-Based Sex Education under the Spotlight of Sexual and Intimate Citizenship: A Focus on Portugal and England*, Porto: FPCEUP.

Santos, S. A. (2018), 'La Ciudadanía Sexual e Íntima como Espacio para el Reconocimiento de la Igualdad Sexual y de Género en la Educación Sexual', in M. Venegas, P. Chacon-Gordilho and A. Fernandez (eds), *De la Igualdade de Género à la Igualdade Sexual y de Género*, 185–203, Madrid: Editorial Dykinson.

Santos, S. A. and E. Macedo (2020), 'Unveiling Silence and Pressures in the Messages of School Sex Education: A Path towards More Egalitarian and Democratic Relationships', in B. E. Grau and C. P. Vieira (eds), *Sexualities, Gender and Violence: A View from the Iberian Peninsula*, 91–109, New York: Nova Science Publishers.

Thomson, R. and S. Scott (1992), *Learning about Sex: Young Women and the Social Construction of Sexual Identity*, London: Tufnell Press.

Weeks, J. (2010), *Sexuality*, London: Routledge.

CHAPTER FIVE

Women's Bodies and Sport: Dialogues with Paulo Freire

Paula Silva, Angelita Alice Jaeger and Grasiela Oliveira

Introduction

It is not possible to study the world, abstracting the body from its place. If we do, something will always be missing. […] The world we see, what we imagine and build, all this is, if we like, corporeal matter. Thought is the body. […] We cannot live without a body nor talk about it without using it.[1]

(PAULO C. SILVA 2015)

The body is the sport's protagonist, and sport, as a cultural manifestation, transforms it. In turn, the body and the social power it generates and emanates induce transformations in the arenas of sport. In this connection, we can mention the conscious body that Paulo Freire discreetly presented in his works. He says: 'As presences in the world, human beings are conscious bodies that transform it, acting and thinking, which allows them to know at a reflective level. Precisely because of this, we can take our presence in the world as an object of critical analysis' (Freire 1981: 87).

As *conscious bodies*, women athletes have a relationship with the world and the territory of sports that they critically analyse. By taking multiple risks, they act and transform the sport, the world, and themselves because 'risk is a necessary ingredient of mobility without which there is no culture or history' (Freire 2000: 30). By doing so, women conquer spaces and visibility, change rules, denounce inequalities, resist and lead new stories, and rewrite sports culture. Women in sports have never been accommodated to the gender order. They have broken down asymmetries and transformed contemporary sports practice (Jaeger et al. 2010) because 'accommodation is the expression of giving up the fight for change' (Freire 2000: 41).

Based on feminist thought in the matching up with Freire, this chapter aims to open dialogues on the role of sport in the conscientization of gender issues and its potential for women's empowerment.

Bodies, gender and sport

The globalization of culture and a growing conscientization of the importance of the body have capitalized on physical and sports activities as one of the most relevant social and cultural practices of our times. Freire describes conscientization as awareness through critical dialogical reflection, which guides transformative action (Macedo et al. 2013).

Sports practice is centred on the athlete's relationship with the body. The body moves, acts, reacts, changes, shapes itself, transgresses, expresses, recovers and transfigures itself to respond to the requests that the practice of sport demands. One can do it with greater or lesser pleasure, more or less effort, and different goals. Sporting bodies take on multiple configurations. They are gendered bodies of different ages and ethnic origins that suffer or enjoy and are more or less qualified. The body that practices sport is a multiplicity of bodies. Nothing exists outside the body. What exists and the perception of the world come to us through our bodies. Not only do we have a body, but we are the body itself (Merleau-Ponty 1999). Freire (1993: 43) also warns that 'what I know, I know with my body: with my critical mind, but also with my feelings, with my intuitions, with my emotions'. Our conscious body critically reads what surrounds it in a dialogic relationship between conscious bodies and their interactions with the world that can result in new worlds, new learning, new subjects, and new bodies.

As Freire and Faundez ([1985] 2014: 20) remind us, 'The human body, old or young, fat or thin, no matter what color, the conscious body, which looks at the stars, is the body that writes, the body that speaks, the body that fights, the body that loves, the body that hates, the body that suffers, the body that dies, the body that lives!' Thus, the body exposed to the gaze reifies social expectations (Almeida 2000). Sporting bodies express and trigger feelings and emotions. But frequently, bodies are contained in their expressions, subjugated in the forms they can present and censored in the movements they produce. Above all, it is the sexual categorization imposed on bodies that limits their experiences and guides their practice of sport more often than we suppose. Consequently, this is how we regress to the discourse of biological difference of an essentialist type, to the unavoidable dichotomy (Almeida 2003) that does not shelter the great diversity inherent to being human.

> The term **dichotomy** refers to the assumption of a division or contrast between two things that are represented as opposed or entirely different. In gender terms, one can refer to the gender dichotomy that represents men and women as opposite sides of the human coin, denying both their common features and the diversity among men and among women.

We do not intend to develop theories or deepen concepts but simply to remind the reader that being a man or a woman is not an acquired state. It is a permanent active construction condition, a *becoming* that involves tensions and ambiguities. As a multidimensional construct, gender is a process that develops throughout life, informed by and presenting several institutional, individual, and relational perspectives. This means that the gender order in a society is appropriated by individuals who, in turn, develop gendered images and gender identities in the process (Pfister 2002).

Gender issues constantly challenge us shrewdly or abruptly and are not always an object of reflection. Many characters played an important role in different knowledge domains, insensitive to these constant interpellations, but this is not the case for the thinker Paulo Freire. Let us consider, albeit briefly, how Paulo Freire was awakened to gender issues during his life as a pedagogue and a man of praxis, as we describe below (see also Chapters 1 and 2 in this book).

Gender concerns in Freire's ideas were raised in the early 1970s by feminists who, sharing some of Freire's positions concerning class relations of domination and subordination, criticized the fact that women were hidden in his texts. Freire's (1992) first reaction to these criticisms consisted of the absurd argument invariably used in the most diverse social and cultural spaces: 'Now when I say man, the woman is necessarily included' (35). But he quickly became aware of how much this argument legitimized gender oppression and identified the false neutral (Barreno

1985), i.e., the use of generic masculine as a guarantee of gender-neutral language. This 'false neutral' is, in fact, a form of discrimination against women: 'Discrimination against women, expressed and made by sexist discourse and embodied in concrete practices, is a colonial way of treating them, and is, therefore, incompatible with any progressive position' (Freire 1992: 35).

Changes in gender issues demand a new ideological positioning that, among others, includes a language change: 'The rejection of the macho ideology, which necessarily implies the recreation of language, is part of the possible dream in favor of changing the world' (Freire 1992: 35). Change implies continuing to analyse gender relations and their singularities in search of undoing gender. In turn, this implies demanding a commitment to a new ideological positioning that supports transformative action.

Girls and boys are actively involved in building gender relations and identities. For girls, the emancipatory potential of practising sport lies in the opportunity to experience power through the body, improve knowledge and motor skills, conquer a sense of mastery of their body, challenge passive constructions of femininity and empower them as women. The potential of body empowerment allows an understanding of the conversion of corporal/physical power to social power (Fisette 2011). Hence, this means:

> using women's lived-body experiences as a litmus against which a physicality construct is evaluated represents a negotiation of this tension between the social and the physical. While both experiences and bodies are culturally and ideologically saturated, the physical experience of the body as lived is also meaningful and influential. Attending to both the social and the physical recognises that while women *have* culturally coded bodies, they also *live* those culturally coded bodies in potentially gender disruptive ways.
>
> (McDermott 2000: 334)

Conscientization and the empowerment of bodies

The importance of the body is indisputable; the body moves, acts, remembers the liberation struggle; the body ultimately desires, points, announces, protests, bows, rises, draws and remakes the world.

(FREIRE [1991] 2006: 92)

A concept that should be invoked here is that of conscientization, which is already referred to above. Freire introduced the relevance of bodily and relational aspects of knowledge, proposing a perspective of awareness of the world beyond the rationalist and cognitivist language on which it was previously based (Freire 1979). Liberating knowledge is no longer exclusively based on rationality. It is present in the process of *conscientization*, in which dialogue is necessary.

> It implies awareness of myself in the world, with it, and with others, which also implies our ability to perceive and understand the world, which cannot be reduced to a rationalist experience. It is as a totality – reason, feelings, emotions, desires – that my body, conscious of the world and myself, captures the world it is intended for.
>
> (Freire 1995: 75)

As a strategy of (re)interpretation of power, like that present in feminist methodologies, the process of *conscientization* aims to provide resources to oppressed groups and assist them in becoming protagonists in their emancipation. Conscientization is a transforming method that associates the claim for justice and equality with knowledge production (Oliveira et al. 2009); it aims to empower people and oppressed/discriminated groups and implies the commitment of social, political and scientific dimensions. Freire criticized and fought social structures to transform them in his engagement with oppressed groups. The view of education as praxis was incorporated by educators who shared Freire's ideas in constructing a fairer and non-oppressive society. This includes feminists in pedagogy who, while recognizing the contribution of Freire's thought, did not ignore the singularities of gender oppression and analysed the patriarchal model to develop a liberating education that specifically supported girls (Weiler 1991, 2001). Several feminist studies analysed the forms of production and contestation of the oppressive construction of a sporting body (e.g., Cox and Thompson 2000; Jaeger and Goellner 2011; Paula Silva, Botelho-Gomes and Goellner 2012), highlighting how difficult it was for women to be included and become a constant presence in the stronghold sports traditionally associated with men (e.g., Velija, Mierzwinski and Fortune 2013).

However, sports emerge as a political space and, especially, as a place of resistance and transformation of gender relations (Hall 2005). To transform sport and the world concerning gender relations, it is necessary to consider the following:

The world is not. The world is being. As a curious, intelligent subjectivity that interferes with the objectivity with which I dialectically relate, my role in the world is not only that of someone who observes what happens but also that of someone who intervenes as a subject of occurrences. I am not only the object of *History* but its subject as well. In history, culture, and politics, *I see* it not *to adapt* to it but *to transform* it.

(Freire 2000: 79)

There are several sports in which women who are aware of the place they have materialize resistance and produce changes. This is the case of mixed martial arts (MMA), a combination of multiple styles of martial arts and sports such as boxing, kickboxing, judo and jiu-jitsu (Hirose and Pih 2010); victory can be achieved by knockout, submission or by decision of the judges (Seungmo et al. 2008). MMA was initially dominated by male athletes, with masculinity extolled and expressed in strong, aggressive, virile, competitive bodies. But women have put on their gloves and entered the octagon to fight with twice the will and determination of their male peers (Hirose and Pih 2010; Silva, Jaeger and Silva 2021). It was officially in 2013 that the UFC (Ultimate Fighting Championship) opened the competition to women. Like those in martial arts, these athletes have only recently begun to be brought out of obscurity. Furthermore, the impact of their attitudes has been increasingly discussed in the sport as they challenge gender norms; empowered by their bodies, women challenge the hegemonic masculinity and emphasize femininity (Follo 2012). In addition, women strongly undermine the traditional idea that sets women's bodies as feeble, weak and passive (Silva et al. 2021).

Conclusion

Nobody leaves their world, entered by their roots, with an empty or dry body. We carry with us the memory of many plots, the wet body of our history, of our culture.

(FREIRE 1992: 32–3)

The dialogues with Paulo Freire's thought reinforce the need to study how bodies, embedded in culture, live and transform their place. From Freire, we expand the empowerment of disadvantaged groups to the study of empowerment by women's bodies in the sports arena. Sports practices can be recognized as strategies, as spaces of appropriation of power and empowerment for change. This is achievable in sports and other areas of women's personal and social lives. Men and women intervene in the world, produce transformations and are transformed by them (Freire 2000).

In sports such as MMA, women athletes challenge gender norms by permanently putting tension on binary and biologized representations. Moreover, they potentiate body architectures. The aggressiveness required in fights suggests a multiplicity of bodies that demands plurality in constructing femininity.

As there is no life in immobility if we are socially responsible, we should not passively accommodate ourselves to societal injustices (Freire 1993). It is more than time to assume that the gender order, as a result of human action, is subject to change (Connell 2015). So, dreaming is mandatory. Walking the path to pursuing change in society, constantly altered, is something that transforms us. It is a route that, at the same time, nourishes and exhausts us. Dreaming is also a political act rooted in human nature in a permanent process of becoming. Therefore, there 'is no change without a dream, like there is no dream without hope' (Freire 1992: 47).

Note

1   All the texts cited in this chapter whose originals are in Portuguese were freely translated.

References

Almeida, M. V. (2000), *Senhores de Si: Uma Interpretação Antropológica da Masculinidade*, Lisboa: Fim de Século.

Almeida, M. V. (2003), 'Antropologia e Sexualidade: Consensos e Conflitos Teóricos Em Perspectiva', in L. Fonseca, C. Soares and J. M. Vaz (eds), *A Sexologia, Perspectiva Multidisciplinar*, 53–72, Coimbra: Quarteto.

Barreno, M. I. (1985), *O Falso Neutro: Um Estudo Sobre a Discriminação Sexual no Ensino*, Lisboa: Instituto de Estudos para o Desenvolvimento.

Connell, R. (2015), 'Gender and Embodiment in World Society', *Revista Lusófona de Estudos Culturais*, 3 (1): 289–95.

Cox, B. and S. Thompson (2000), 'Multiple Bodies: Sportswomen, Soccer and Sexuality', *International Review for the Sociology of Sport*, 35 (1): 5–20.

Fisette, J. L. (2011), 'Exploring How Girls Navigate Their Embodied Identities in Physical Education', *Physical Education and Sport Pedagogy*, 16 (2): 179–96.

Follo, G. (2012), 'A Literature Review of Women and the Martial Arts: Where Are We Right Now?', *Sociology Compass*, 6 (9): 707–17.

Freire, P. (1979), *Conscientização: Teoria e Prática da Libertação: Uma introdução ao Pensamento de Paulo Freire*, São Paulo: Cortez & Moraes.

Freire, P. (1981), *Ação Cultural para a Liberdade e Outros Escritos*, 5th edn, Rio de Janeiro: Paz e Terra.

Freire, P. ([1991] 2006), *A Educação na Cidade*, São Paulo: Cortez.

Freire, P. (1992), *Pedagogia da Esperança: Um Reencontro com a Pedagogia do Oprimido*, Rio de Janeiro: Paz e Terra.

Freire, P. (1993), *Política e Educação*, São Paulo: Cortez.

Freire, P. (1995), *À Sombra desta Mangueira*, São Paulo: Livraria Nova Sede.

Freire, P. (2000), *Pedagogia da Indignação: Cartas Pedagógicas e Outros Escritos*, São Paulo: UNESP.

Freire, P. and A. Faundez ([1985] 2014), *Por uma Pedagogia da Pergunta*, Rio de Janeiro: Paz e Terra.

Hall, A. (2005), 'From Pre- to Postfeminism: A Four-Decade Journey', in P. Markula (ed), *Feminist Sport Studies: Sharing Experiences of Joy and Pain*, 45–61, New York: State University of New York Press.

Hirose, A. and K. Pih (2010), 'Men Who Strike and Men Who Submit: Hegemonic and Marginalized Masculinities in Mixed Martial Arts', *Men and Masculinities*, 13 (2): 190–209.

Jaeger, A. and S. Goellner (2011), 'O Músculo Estraga a Mulher? A Produção de Feminilidades no Fisiculturismo', *Revista Estudos Feministas*, 19 (3): 955–76.

Jaeger, A., P. Botelho-Gomes, P. Silva and S. Goellner (2010), 'Trajetórias de Mulheres no Esporte em Portugal: Assimetrias, Resistências e Possibilidades', *Movimento*, 16 (1): 245–67.

Macedo, E., L. Vasconcelos, M. Evans, M. Lacerda and M. V. Pinto (2013), *Revisitando Paulo Freire: Sentidos na Educação*, Brasília: Liber Livro.

McDermott, L. (2000), 'A Qualitative Assessment of the Significance of Body Perception to Women's Physical Activity Experiences: Revisiting Discussion of Physicalities', *Sociology of Sport Journal*, 17 (4): 331–63.

Merleau-Ponty, M. (1999), *Fenomenologia da Percepção*, São Paulo: Martins Fontes.

Oliveira, J., S. Neves, C. Nogueira and M. Koning (2009), 'Present but Un-named: Feminist Liberation Psychology in Portugal', *Feminism & Psychology*, 19 (3): 394–406.

Pfister, G. (2002), 'Sport and Socialisation: A Gender Perspective', Presentation on the Seminar Idrett Mellom Moral, Politikk of Profit, Lysebu, 22–24 November.

Seungmo, K., T. C. Greenwell, D. Andrew, J. Lee and D. Mahony (2008), 'An Analysis of Spectator Motives in an Individual Combat Sport: A Study of Mixed Martial Arts Fans', *Sport Marketing Quarterly*, 17 (2): 109–19.

Silva, G., A. Jaeger and P. Silva (2021), 'Discursos de Estudantes de Licenciatura em Desporto acerca das Mulheres Atletas de Artes Marciais Mistas', *Movimento*, 27 (1): e27037.

Silva, P. C. (2015), 'Lugar do Conhecimento', *Jornal de Letras*, 5 March. Available online: https://visao.sapo.pt/jornaldeletras/ideiasjl/2015-03-05-lugar-do-conhecimentof812268/.

Silva, P., P. Botelho-Gomes and S. Goellner (2012), 'Masculinities and Sport: The Emphasis on Hegemonic Masculinity in Portuguese Physical Education Classes', *International Journal of Qualitative Studies in Education*, 25 (3): 269–91.

Velija, P., M. Mierzwinski and L. Fortune (2013), '"It Made Me Feel Powerful": Women's Gendered Embodiment and Physical Empowerment in the Martial Arts', *Leisure Studies*, 32 (5): 524–41.

Weiler, K. (1991), 'Freire and a Feminist Pedagogy of Difference', *Harvard Educational Review*, 61 (4): 449–75.

Weiler, K. (2001), 'Rereading Paulo Freire', in K. Weiler (ed), *Feminist Engagements: Reading, Resisting and Revisioning Male Theorists in Education and Cultural studies*, 67–87, New York and London: Routledge Falmer.

PART THREE

From Violence and Oppression to Equity and Transformation

In the Quest for Equity: Violence Against Women and Conscientization through Dialogue

Monica Riutort and Sandra Rupnarain

If the structure does not permit dialogue the structure must be changed

(PAULO FREIRE, AS CITED IN AGER AND AGER 2015)

Introduction[1]

The Peel Institute on Violence Prevention has been reviewing the ongoing prevalence of violence against women in the region of Peel, as well as in Canada, and discovered that violence against women has decreased by a small percentage during the last thirty years despite a large influx of funds from all sectors of government into services and programmes. So why is it still happening? Why is the decrease not comparable to the resources expended? What strategies do we need to revise? What new approach do we need to consider? These questions are at the forefront as we tentatively embark on the development of new approaches and answers.

Oppression politics would suggest that violence against women remains without change due to the short-term, crisis-oriented, paternalistic and fatalistic approach in Canadian dogmata and politics, which can be unintentionally reinforced by Canadian women in positions of power as decision-makers and service providers. These influences continue to keep women in an inequitable relationship of power to men and consequently impact the social and political organizations that represent women who are experiencing violence and healing from violence.

This chapter will attempt to articulate an alternative liberating political equity perspective for survivors of violence adapted from Paulo Freire's educational philosophy, theory and praxis, which he outlined in *Pedagogy of the Oppressed* (Freire [1968] 2000). This project will develop an alternative network of support services that will focus on social and political transformation for women through conscientization, dialogue, critical reflection and collective action (Schugurensky 2014). These concepts are taken from an influential work of Paulo Freire, whose theory serves as a pillar of anti-oppressive practice proposed in this chapter.

For this chapter, inequity is defined as the differences in social and health status among population groups deemed unfair, unjust or preventable, as well as socially produced and systematic in their distribution across the population (World Health Organization 2008). Inequities generally exist along two major gradients: socio-economic status and geographic status (e.g., urban vs. rural location). Inequities also appear to be differences across ethnicity, gender, age and abilities (Provincial Health Services Authority 2011).

The issue of violence against women was brought to the public spotlight by Margaret Mitchell, a member of the Canadian Parliament, when, in 1982, she accidentally caused a ruckus in the House of Commons that sparked national awareness of domestic violence. She told the House of Commons that one in ten Canadian husbands regularly beat their wives. The male Members of the Canadian Parliament (MPs) erupted in laughter and shouted, to which she furiously replied: 'This is no laughing matter.' Ms Mitchell brought the question of domestic violence into the open. Before this time, people in Canada had not addressed the subject of violence in the home. Police did not check out reported cases of abuse. It was just a silent topic. But the next day, after people had seen the incident and her angry reaction on TV, hundreds of people, men and women, got in touch with their MPs, objecting to this attitude towards battered women (White 2015). Public pressure widely responded, and the media coverage prompted a House of Commons report on domestic violence from the Standing Committee on Health (Vollman, Anderson and McFarlane 2008). Thirty-three years since this incident in the House of Commons, and under the pressure of Canadian citizens, particularly the active women's movement, the government of Canada has spent millions of dollars to pursue a whole range of strategies to deal with violence against women in Canada.

The government cannot stop violence against women on its own. In 2021 there were 127,082 victims of police-reported family violence in Canada, which includes violence committed by spouses, parents, children, siblings and extended family members, and represents a rate of 336 victims per 100,000 population. This marked the fifth consecutive year of increase. Women and girls represented two-thirds (69%) of family violence victims. The rate of family violence was more than two times higher for women and girls than for men and boys, 457 victims *versus* 212 per 100,000 population (Statistics Canada 2022).

At the macro level, in its study of the economic costs of spousal violence against women, the Department of Justice found that the overall cost of spousal violence against women and men was estimated at $7.4 billion. The cost of spousal violence against women specifically was estimated at

$4.8 billion (Zhang et al. 2013). Across Canada, the estimated economic cost to the justice system was $545.2 million (Sinha 2013).

In March 2013, the Peel Committee on Sexual Assault (PCSA), an advisory committee of services providers, hosted 'Café Scientifique: An Open Discussion of the Experiences of Immigrant and Racialized Women Survivors of Sexual Assault in Accessing Primary Health Care Services'. The purpose of this event was to uncover the barriers to accessing primary healthcare services for immigrant and racialized female survivors of sexual assault. A group of empowering panellists with expertise in sexual assault openly discussed their personal experiences. Among the panellists were women survivors of violence, service providers from both social and health sectors, and researchers in violence against women. The Café created opportunities for meaningful dialogue.

The discussion brought to the forefront women's experiences of dealing with existing government services, which were identified as paternalistic, with a culturally incompetent approach. Services and programmes are more focused on immediate crises; they are short-term and do not include the application of social determinants to the unique experience of each survivor. As it exists today, the system seems to provide little opportunity for women to have a thorough discourse, critical reflection and analysis, and engagement in collective action.

One important outcome of the Café was the recognition among participants that violence against women is an issue of human rights and a global issue. Every year, violence in the home and the community devastates the lives of millions of women who are beaten, coerced into sex or otherwise abused. Violence against women is rooted in a global culture of discrimination that denies women equal rights with men and legitimizes the appropriation of women's bodies for individual gratification or political ends (Amnesty International 2017). Violence against women is additionally compounded by further discrimination as it relates to race, ethnicity, sexual identity, social status, class and age. Such multiple forms of discrimination restrict women's choices, increase their vulnerability to violence and reinforce the barriers that make it difficult for women to obtain justice.

The participants agreed that the state has a fiduciary responsibility to protect individuals from human rights abuses and to prevent and protect women against interpersonal violence. Their unified suggestion was that it is time to move from a paralysing and paternalistic state approach, which is keeping women in a *status quo* situation, to an active women's participation in liberation from violence through an understanding of the causes of political, social and economic structures of domination that keep women in a state of oppression. These were identified as social processes that collective action can challenge and overcome.

Café Scientifique 2013 marked the beginning of the Peel Institute on Violence Prevention (PIVP) as it exemplified a gathering where academics, service providers, and survivors came together to discuss the current services, identify issues of concern and share ideas about moving forward more seamlessly. Following the Café, a proposal to establish the PIVP was created. This proposal was approved for funding by the Ontario Trillium Foundation and is administered by Family Services of Peel (namely, by the Peel Committee on Sexual Assault 2013).

PIVP is an interdisciplinary and intersectoral collaborative initiative among agencies in the region of Peel, Ontario, Canada, working to eradicate all forms of violence. Operating within an equity lens and an anti-oppressive, anti-racist framework, the PIVP is a focal point for data-driven, evidence-informed practice, which will improve the organization of services, combining the perspectives of the diverse population served, academia and community service providers. The PIVP is bringing under one roof survivors of violence, service providers, policymakers, and substantial scientific evidence to transform the culture of how services and programmes for survivors of violence are created, provided and evaluated in Peel. The robust evidence we collect and analyse will benefit decision-making at Peel's community, policy and service levels.

The research on violence prevention by the PIVP focuses on all types of violence for the following at-risk groups: youth, seniors, women, the aboriginal population, people with disabilities and male victims of violence. The data collected by PIVP will enable agencies to (a) be more effective in their evaluation of the impact and effectiveness of their services; (b) support the re-structuring and adapting of their services and programmes to be more focused on survivors' needs; and (c) enable agencies to provide a more seamless and person-centred response.

To respond to the collective voices of the women from the *Café Scientifique*, the first task of the institute was to conduct a thorough regional scan of the organizations providing services for survivors of violence in Peel. The second task was to identify the population of clients receiving services. The third task was to identify the type of services provided, how, what data was collected about these services, and what kind of communication and coordination existed between them.

The first pilot study by the PIVP was 'Identifying Gaps in Data Collection Practice of Health, Justice and Social Service Agencies Serving Survivors of Interpersonal Violence'. Using mixed methods, we worked to understand the scope of services available and survey data collection practices of a cohort of agencies providing services for survivors of violence in Peel.

The studied population was service providers working with survivors of interpersonal violence (SOIV) as defined by the WHO (2010; domestic violence and sexual assault).

A regional scan, survey questionnaire and interviews were used to answer the research questions. During the scanning, seventy-nine organizations were identified as key stakeholders (or essential service providers) in the spectrum of community service agencies supporting victims of violence. Twenty-five organizations were identified as providing direct services to survivors. Of those twenty-five organizations, twelve were selected for face-to-face interviews and survey questionnaires. Out of the twelve organizations selected, one is a smaller ethnic-specific agency with minimal staff and resources, and the other eleven have many staff and resources. The questionnaire consisted of the following:

1. **Demographic Data:** To provide a picture of the demographics of those using the services with a particular focus on social determinants, fifty-two variables of social determinants were standardized with Statistics Canada, which were covered by Census Profile, 2011, and NHS Profile (National Household Survey), 2011.

2. **Health Data:** Four variables: does or does not have a GP/family doctor, medical history, present health condition, etc.

3. **Violence/Abuse Details & History:** Four variables: type of violence/abuse that is the reason for the current visit, history of violence/abuse, type of previous violence/abuse, and any treatment and action(s) taken.

4. **Services Used:** Eighteen variables: accessing other healthcare providers for a current reason or other reasons, accessing other social services providers for a current reason or other reasons, accessing other legal or justice services providers for a current reason or other reasons, if there are any health services desired but not accessing, if there are any social services desired but not accessing and if there are any legal or justice services desired but not accessing.

5. **Data about Services offered:** Forty-four variables for types of services offered for survivors of interpersonal violence have been standardized with Statistics Canada, which were covered by the victim services survey and offered directly by victim service agencies in 2014.

The interviews methodology

The interviews were recorded and subsequently transcribed for qualitative analysis. The interview transcripts were analysed using a thematic analysis approach (Strauss and Corbin 1990). Although grounded theory principles of qualitative analysis were applied, our data was more structured around certain specific domains as previously detailed and ideas were delineated, and themes were generated within each. Following the classic methodology of this thematic approach, ideas were coded and grouped to give categories and more general themes. Ideally, data collection and analysis would continue until reaching a point of data saturation.

Results of the pilot study

The study indicated that agencies predominantly collected data to satisfy government requirements for financial support. There is inconsistency in data collection by agencies. Because of the absence of key demographic variables in the agency's data collection practices, the provision of services is predominantly episodic.

All informants wanted the system to work better to serve the community and offered a range of ideas for improvement. Information collection was seen as important, and data sharing is seen as a form of communicating and relating around service provision. The barrier to sharing between agencies is linked to confidentiality. The informants do not seem to be clear on what the 'circle of care' or 'referral loops' are and how they relate to the interest of the service recipients. The collected data demonstrated that agencies work in silos. The rate of drops between agencies is unknown but is likely higher than people realize.

Other findings included:

1. The predominant focus of data collection is to satisfy funders' requirements.

2. Inconsistencies in data collection practices among agencies.

3. Absence of key demographic variables in the data collection practices of agencies.

4. Services are provided in the absence of data.

5. Predominantly episodic incident-based service provision.

6. Absence of critical person-focused assessments.

7. Collective desire to improve data collection practices and move forward standardization.

8. Siloed approach to service provision.

9. Lack of collective action and education role of services.

In conclusion, the study undertaken by the PIVP confirmed some of the comments heard at the *Café Scientifique* and added some new pieces of information, which allow a greater understanding of the issues in service delivery for SOIV. This study also helped to understand how the organization and delivery of services can be changed to benefit the clients.

Tentative elements to a new approach to services delivery and organization

The issue of violence is addressed repeatedly in Paulo Freire's writing. He wrote about divide and rule as a fundamental dimension of the theory of oppressive action, which he said is as old as oppression itself (Freire [1968] 2000). As the oppressor minority subordinates and dominates the majority, it must divide and keep it divided to remain in power. Accordingly, the oppressor halts any method (including violence), any action which, in even incipient fashion, could awaken the oppressed need for unity. Only in his writing to his niece Cristina, he addressed violence against women as political prisoners whose torture included rape (Freire 1996).

Freire was also concerned about children being raised with a misconception of freedom and their violent acts towards others (screaming, writing on walls, killing animals and the like) (Freire 2004). He also addressed what he called the strange notion of 'killing an Indian [*sic*]'[2] for play and the intolerable perversity of young men who dehumanize themselves, perpetrating such acts. Moreover, Freire refers to two determinants of health, race and gender, which are central dimensions of oppression and such to inclusion and exclusion on individual in society. Finally, on the issue of racism and *machismo*, he said:

> The problem I have with racist people is not the color of their skin but rather the color of their ideology. Likewise, my difficulty with the macho does not rest in their sex but in their discriminatory ideology. Being racist or macho, progressive or reactionary, is not an integral part of human nature but rather is an orientation toward being more.
>
> (Freire 1978: 86)

Paulo Freire was a man of his time. He lived between 1921 and 1997. He lived through major events of the twentieth century, including the Great Depression, Second World War and, in the context of Latin America, the populism and developmentalism of the 1950s, the revolutionary movements and military coups of the 1960s and 1970s, the return to democracy in the 1980s and neoliberalism in the 1990s. Paulo Freire was relevant to the twentieth century and his theory is still applicable to the twenty-first century and particularly relevant to violence against women in Canada today (Schugurensky 2014).

Developmentalism was a Eurocentric, anthropocentric and economistic logic said to serve to 'guide' the 'young nations'. It builds on the opposition between 'so-called' developed and underdeveloped countries, leading to relations of domination/subordination between countries. The values of economy overreach the human value.

Services for survivors of violence in Canada are also a reflection of our times. In 1995, Mike Harris was elected the province's premier of Ontario. He brought what he called the 'Common Sense Revolution' as part of the popular neoliberal political model. Harris changed the relationship between government and those organizations and individuals who depend on the government for support. The idea that civil society should be seen as a partner of government in building a better society was replaced by a new idea: that civil society should be regarded as parasitic, whose fate depends on the grace and favor of government (Hennessy 2015).

The **neoliberal political model** is centred on politics and economics. It values private enterprises and the transfer of control of economic factors from governments to the private sector. Guided by the market, it is concerned about the efficiency of free market and focused on reducing government expenditure and regulation, as well as about public ownership.

This notion that organizations providing services to vulnerable people are 'parasitic' has set down deep roots in government and established a polarized, cultural dynamic between funders and community leaders of transfer—payment agencies and the people they serve. This dynamic is only one small step away from directly blaming vulnerable people for needing government support in the first place.

This is all part of an industrial-age, capitalist-based worldview that says simply: 'All people are created equal, and your success or failure is entirely dependent on your effort and ability' (BBWON 2015: 10). Therefore, if you need help, you are weak and automatically cast as a less-valued member of society. Our systems clearly reflect these attitudes and beliefs. Although in Canada, we have sometimes tried to balance them with a social safety net, this support is being steadily eroded by those who are more comfortable blaming individuals for their life situations. We need to correct our perceptions and adjust our systems to reflect the twenty-first-century reality that we are social beings who are interconnected and interdependent. And this is where the *Pedagogy of the Oppressed* offers a method to restore the balance. For Freire, it is the people who are pushed to the margins of society who can help us find our way because they have direct experience of how the system does not work (and are the least invested in maintaining it). We need them to understand and transform, 'and we need each other' (BBWON 2015).

The suggestion is to reinvent Paulo Freire's theory and praxis to develop a new integrated approach to delivering services for survivors of violence. Well-coordinated services with solid communication strategies will integrate the following aspect of Freire's theory:

1. A new role for the service provider is not only a counsellor or facilitator but also an educator. An educator who understands the role of education in social transformation.

2. An educator who can play a key role in social change by nurturing, through dialogue, a survivor of violence – critical consciousness and transformative collective praxis.

3. An educator who challenges oppression and nurtures liberation.

4. Development of support services that are universal and transdisciplinary in nature – different disciplinary backgrounds, different ideological and epistemological backgrounds.

5. Services that emerge from the concrete experience of marginalized people and cemmunities.

6. In the Quest for Equity: Violence against Women and Conscientization through dialogue from a paternalistic to a symbiotic relation with government.

Final remarks

In our quest for equity and social justice, we will aim for full humanization, calling for hope, a vision of utopia and faith in social changes. We could then move away from paternalism and become true agents of change, establishing a relationship of mutual collaboration with others.

Notes

1   Acknowledgement: Olha Oliynyk and Isha Chaudhary, volunteers with the Institute for their time (reading and editing).
2   Killing 'the Indian' are words taking directly from Paulo Freire. Beyond the inadmissible idea of 'killing' a human being, these words are politically incorrect today. A more inclusive way to refer to the formerly called 'Indian' would be 'Indigenous peoples'.

References

Ager, A. and J. Ager (2015), *Faith, Secularism, and Humanitarian Engagement*, New York: Palgrave Macmillan.

Amnesty International (2017), 'Violence against Women', *Amnesty International*, 19 May. Available online: https://www.amnestyusa.org/themes/womens-rights/violence-against-women/.

Building a Bigger Wave Ontario Network (2015), 'Ontario's New Roundtable on Violence against Women', *Provincial VAWCC* Newsletter, Summer: 1–23. https://cdn.prod.website-files.com/639a353b13ed06586953bcf1/63bc4ddf78495ee4785dcab3_BBWON_Newsletter_-_Summer_2015.pdf.

Freire, P. ([1968] 2000), *Pedagogy of the Oppressed*, New York: Continuum.

Freire, P. (1978), *Pedagogy of the Heart*, New York: Continuum.

Freire, P. (1996), *Letters to Cristina: Reflections on My Life and Work*, New York: Routledge.

Freire, P. (2004), *Pedagogy of Indignation*, Boulder, CO: Paradigm.

Hennessy, T. (2015), 'Assessing the Common-Sense Revolution, 20 Years Later', *On Policy, The Canadian Centre for Policy Alternatives' Ontario Office*, Summer: 8–9. https://policyalternatives.ca/sites/default/files/uploads/publications/Ontario%20Office/2015/06/Ontario%20Policy%20magazine%20-%20Summer%202015-%20final.pdf.

Provincial Health Services Authority (2011), *Towards Reducing Health Inequities: A Health System Approach to Chronic Disease Prevention. A Discussion Paper*, Vancouver, BC: Population & Public Health, Provincial Health Services Authority.

Schugurensky, D. (2014), *Paulo Freire*, London: Bloomsbury.

Sinha, M., ed (2013), *Measuring Violence against Women: Statistical Trends*, Kanata: Canadian Centre for Justice Statistics.

Statistics Canada (2022), Victims of Police-Reported Family and Intimate Partner Violence in Canada, 2021. 11 July. Available online: https://www150.statcan.gc.ca/n1/daily-quotidien/221019/dq221019c-eng.htm.

Strauss, A. and J. M. Corbin (1990), *Basics of Qualitative Research: Grounded Theory Procedures and Techniques*, Newbury Park, CA: Sage.

Vollman, A., E. Anderson and J. McFarlane (2008), *Canadian Community as Partner*, Philadelphia, PA: Wolters Kluwer Health, Lippincott Williams & Wilkins.

White, N. (2015), 'MPs Laughed When She Spoke on Battered Women', *Toronto Star*, 13 June. Available online: http://www.thestar.com/life/2008/06/13/mps_laughed_when_she_spoke_on_battered_women.html.

World Health Organization (2008), *Commission on the Social Determinants of Health, 2005–2008*. Available online: https://www.who.int/initiatives/action-on-the-social-determinants-of-health-for-advancing-equity/world-report-on-social-determinants-of-health-equity/commission-on-social-determinants-of-health.

World Health Organization (2010), *Preventing Intimate Partner and Sexual Violence against Women: Taking Action and Generating Evidence*, Geneva: World Health Organization. http://www.who.int/reproductïzivehealth/publications/violence/9789241564007/en/.

Zhang, T., J. Hoddenbagh, S. McDonald and K. Scrim (2013), *An Estimation of the Economic Impact of Spousal Violence in Canada, 2009*, Ottawa: Department of Justice Canada.

CHAPTER SEVEN

So that Oppressed Women won't Dream of Becoming the Oppressors

Nilma Renildes da Silva

When a woman [as well as a man] understands her reality, she can raise hypotheses about the challenge of this reality and seek solutions. Thus, it's possible to transform it...

(FREIRE 1979: 30–1)

The invitation of the Paulo Freire Institute Portugal through my dear friend Eunice Macedo, a tireless Freirean researcher, to publish, in English,[1] this chapter about violence against women reminded me of the sad moment that humanity was going through – little by little walking away from the pandemic of Covid-19. I'm sorry for so many victims!

Paulo Freire used to say that we make the road by walking. I saw him so many times walking through the halls of PUC/SP-BR, and I kept thinking: professor, we already had the path to avoiding so many deaths, sequels and so much sadness! I sighed; nostalgia for the times when political/scientific militancy filled me with enthusiasm for studies and courage to seek the strength to reread Freire's ([1992] 2011) book *Pedagogy of Hope: Reliving Pedagogy of the Oppressed.*

With these underlying concerns, I share some data I've collected on the Institute of Applied Economic Research (IPEA) website,[2] focused on femicides (Cerqueira 2021): from 2009 to 2019, 50,056 women were murdered in Brazil. In 2019, 3.737 women were victims of violence, and 1.246 were victims of violence inside their own homes! To be highlighted that 66 per cent of the total were Black women. In this chapter, unfortunately, we won't discuss the sad exponential growth of the victims, such as children, adolescents, vulnerable women, Indigenous and LGBTQIAPN+. Essentially, in capitalist-mediated relationships, those who perpetrate violence against women are, in most cases, men, bosses, partners and ex-spouses.

The acronym **LGBTQIAPN+** refers to sexual affective diversity, including Lesbian, Gay, Bi, Trans, Queer/Questioning, Intersex, Asexual/Aromantic/Agender, Pan/Poly, Non-binary and more.

According to Melo (2021: 351), 'Brazil fails to comply with the obligation to establish a favorable policy to allow the fully exercise of the right to information on femicides, which assumes a social and instrumental dimension to the implementation of other women's rights.' As stated above, we do not have an official union body to guarantee transparency, *scientificity* and reliability in statistics on the reality of violence against women, nor to highlight the actual number of cases and types of violence that are nationally underreported. Here is a breach not only of the Inter-American Court of Human Rights agreements concerning the Claude Reys *vs.* Chile precedent but of all our laws protecting children, Blacks, Indigenous people, women, the LGBTQIAPN+ community and people with disabilities.

After so many international conventions for eliminating violence against women, of which our country is a signatory, we witness a frightening setback in the legal guarantees of all kinds of rights for women and other strata of society. This takes place in a historical moment when many women already understood themselves as bearers of rights and reported feeling like women and not like exploited victims oppressed by domestic life.

It is worth mentioning that Paulo Freire's political/scientific option has always been from the perspective of the oppressed who, according to him, may perceive the immediate reasons for their suffering (the appearance of the facts) without, however, capturing all the inherent complexity of this very fact (its essence) (Freire [1975] 2021). The same happens to women who are victims of domestic violence. The fact that they may not understand the complexity of the relationships that permeate the use of violence means that they do not report it, leading to underreporting of cases and women remaining in relationships that violate them daily. This comes together with their fear of added violence due to reporting. The subjugation of women is a phenomenon that comes from the establishment of patriarchy and is reaffirmed in current capitalism through heteronormativity, racism and misogyny (Macedo 2015).

Letting go of abusive relationships goes beyond recognizing yourself in it and all its implications; it extends to social issues. In this sense, we must insist on understanding the position of women as victims and the advantage from which capitalism benefits. As already referred to by Saffioti (1978), the oppression of women continues to be an instrument that allows capitalists to manage the entire workforce. In this system, the social place ascribed to women is of victims of structural violence, mediated by capitalism to reproduce its mode of production and reproduction.

In Brazil, to deal with the complexity of violence against women and curb it, there are two main laws; first, Law 11.340/2006, known as Maria da Penha Law, which creates mechanisms to reduce domestic and family violence against women under article 226 of the Federal Constitution (Brazil 1988), the Convention on the Elimination of All Forms of Discrimination against Women (Brazil 2002), and the Inter-American Convention to Prevent, Punish and Eradicate Violence against Women (Brazil 1996); this law also provides for the creation of Courts for Domestic and Family Violence against Women; amends the Criminal Procedure Code (Brazil 1941), the Penal Code (Brazil 1940) and the Penal Execution Law (Brazil 1984); and takes other measures.

The second, more recent, is Law 13.104/2015, the Feminicide Law, which classifies femicide as a heinous crime with aggravating factors when it happens in specific situations of vulnerability (pregnancy, minor, in the presence of children, etc.). The law characterizes violent intentional lethality by sex condition. There is femicide when the aggression involves domestic and family violence, or when it shows contempt or discrimination against the condition of a woman, and even when the aggression is committed against a female person within the victim's family that intentionally causes injuries or health problems leading to their death (Waiselfisz 2015).

In this sense, my option for an action that fosters women's potential to search for consciousness-in-itself and for-itself and freedom was greatly inspired by the work of Paulo Freire.

Working for the elimination of violence against women through historical–cultural psychology

Freire's work is based on my ethical–political principles since I had contact with his work before my academic training in psychology. As I became a professor/researcher in psychology, I appropriated the cultural–historical theory, and my performance/action, from then on, could count on other theorists and thinkers. Throughout this chapter, I will mention some fundamentals for developing my work.

I am certain that scientific knowledge is not exempt from the reproduction of ideological discourses; racist, misogynistic discourses often reproduce structural violence. This includes psychological science, which commonly produces specific ways of thinking about the human psyche. This means certain contents may be reinforced and circulated in the social fabric, restoring oppressive and anti-democratic practices. Freire ([1975] 2011: 94) denounced 'the discrimination of women [...] made by the sexist discourse is a colonial way of treating it, [...] incompatible, therefore, with any progressive position'.

An important aspect to underline is that technologies have brought great benefits to the socialization of knowledge. Still, we await the maturation of social networks regarding the circulation of content stripped of violence and the dominant ideology. However, one cannot deny that access to scientific production and knowledge exchange has advanced somewhat. The contents of feminist studies produced by women of different ethnicities became more accessible, and this vast work is plentiful in my practice.

With Sueli Carneiro (2002, 2004), Lelia Gonzalez (2020) and others, we learned to talk and demand better conditions for the Black population in Brazil and Latin America. With Neuza de Souza Santos (2021), we discovered what it is like to live the psychic experience of being Black/exploited from colonization to today and throughout our day. Little by little, we also seek Black and Indigenous people's artistic and literary production, revealing our *escrevivências*[3] and decolonizing our bibliographic references. Thus, we follow Freire's ([1975] 2021) *somo selo* concept that refers to the development of cultural action for freedom, enabling, whenever possible, a critical understanding of reality and giving new meanings to our community dealings and change.

In turn, Silvia Lane (1984), Martin-Baró (1989) and the theory of the group process as a method of action and research allow us to verify the personal and collective interests, i.e., the question of power, since the group process is characterized by the categories: identity, activity and power. In this sense, it is possible to organize women to face violent situations, strengthening them for life!

In addition to unveiling the dominant ideology, identified as crucial by Freire ([1968] 2014) and Martin-Baró (1989), that places women in daily subordination, we also make recourse to Leontiev's (1978) 'activity' category. This theoretical scope supports the discussion in the groups, allowing them to (i) understand the reasons why women remain in relationships that cause them so much suffering and mortification, (ii) talk with them about the historical conditions that keep them imprisoned in this way of living and (iii) fostering the possibility of metamorphosing[4] themselves and seek for new characters for their identities.

The women, together and in proximity to the group process, analyse their daily actions, procedures to complete their activities and what needs to be modified. Such references also help us list the actions and operations necessary for changes in their daily lives and to perceive the transformations in their consciousness about their psychosocial condition; in other words, the passage from a state of dehumanization (associated with real consciousness) to a critical, humanized consciousness that speeds up change (Freire [1975] 2021).

The *human development of psychism* historical–cultural theory, by Vygotsky (2000), has been fundamental also to working with oppressed women facing violence. These discussions with women allow for denaturalizing life stages and strengthening the fundamental activities of each period of human development. At the same time, they are supported in reinterpreting this knowledge for their children's education and social coexistence.

Thus, we are concomitantly deconstructing notions rooted both in everyday life and in classical theories about women, and we question some theoretical positions that do not encompass the contradictions of gender and ethnicity in the discussion of social classes, for we understand that it is not possible to think these questions in traditional logic. Only dialectical logic, in the relation between the *universal, particular* and *singular* (Oliveira 2005), can offer a movement of thought that makes accessible the articulation of all the contradictions present in violence against women.

At the current historical moment, it is not possible to think about the apparent and singular phenomenon of women's conditions except as a synthesis of multiple determinations arising from the particularity of the capitalist mode of production. This means that even if the system did not lock women inside their houses to be beaten or killed, this fact is somewhat advantageous for its maintenance and for the extraction of more and more surplus value from human labour.

The subject of women and their oppression is not subjective and a petty-bourgeois or bourgeois issue, nor are we fragmenting the class struggle as a starting point for women's struggles. The fight against women's oppression has its starting and ending points in the class struggle, a relationship that brings together Freire's thoughts and some lines of feminism.[5]

However, the root of women's oppression cannot be sought only in itself. Psychologizing their experiences is extremely necessary so that women can elaborate on their psychic sufferings. Still, seeking the root of this very social structure that engenders and maintains such suffering is primal. It is in the real and concrete world, in the social fabric, that women's oppression develops daily. In Brazil, since post-enslavement, a genocide of the Black population has been perpetrated; this fact has implications for the interpretation of domestic violence, especially in the field of psychosocial care.

Women do not exist abstractly; they live in concrete societies marked by oppression. In this sense, no struggle for the emancipation of women takes place outside the class struggle, namely because we cannot escape the particular mediation imposed by the empire of capital. Consequently, the emancipation of women will elevate the class struggle because only emancipated individuals will be able to build the revolutionary process, not the individuals subject to the daily alienation.

So that oppressed women won't dream of becoming the oppressors

By general considerations, it is necessary to go further, moving towards women's freedom and the constant search for substantive equality between men and women, as Mészáros (2002) points out, *deprivatized*, without heteronormative and racist standards. It is also imperative to *deprivatize* relations within the social division of labour and the division of the social labour, inside and outside the home.

The condition of women victims of domestic violence and harassment[6] is always a limit situation that completely escapes from our control and in which empirical existence is halted and brought to an aporetic state. It is worth mentioning that Jaspers (1993) pioneered the concept of limit situation, which Freire also used in several works.

Therefore, we must keep summoning the struggle for emancipation and freedom. As Paulo Freire ([1968] 2014, [1975] 2021, [1992] 2011) defends, only then it is possible to free women from oppression and build social relationships that are not permeated using violence. So that the dream of the oppressed women will not be to become the oppressors, we must rescue the Freirean path. I finish my text by inviting readers to learn the totality of Freire's thought, synthesized in the categories of unity, community experience and the full exercise of humanity.

Notes

1   Acknowledgements: My affectionate thanks to Marilia Duka, my daughter, for her collaboration in translating this chapter.
2   https://www.ipea.gov.br/atlasviolencia/arquivos/artigos/1375-atlasdaviolencia2021completo.pdf.
3   Concept developed by Conceição Evaristo (n.d.), an afro descendent Brazilian academic and writer, to point out a double movement: the life that is written in the experience of each person and the writing of each one in their confrontation with the world; it has an ethical dimension, insofar as it allows the author to assume the place of enunciation of a collective self, of someone who evokes, through their own narrative and voice, the story of a shared 'we'. This term comes from a meaning of subject centred in afro descendent conceptions; therefore, it won't be translated.
4   Concept created by Ciampa (2001) to discuss identity as a category in constant transformation, which replaces the term 'personality', understood by the author as static.
5   For a better understanding, see this book's first chapter by Eunice Macedo.
6   The discussion about harassment is extremely important, especially at this historic moment. However, given its scale it goes beyond the scope of this chapter.

References

Brazil (1940), Decreto-lei n.º 2.848, de 7 de dezembro de 1940. Available online: http://www.planalto.gov.br/ccivil_03/decreto-lei/del2848compilado.htm.

Brazil (1941), Decreto-lei n.º 3.689, de 3 de outubro de 1941. Available online: http://www.planalto.gov.br/ccivil_03/decreto-lei/del3689.htm.

Brazil (1984), Lei n.º 7.210, de 11 de julho de 1984. Available online: http://www.planalto.gov.br/ccivil_03/leis/l7210.htm.

Brazil (1988), *Constituição da República Federativa do Brasil de 1988*. Available online: http://www.planalto.gov.br/ccivil_03/constituicao/constituicao.htm.

Brazil (1996), Decreto n.º 1.973, de 1.º de agosto de 1996. Available online: http://www.planalto.gov.br/ccivil_03/decreto/1996/d1973.htm.

Brazil (2002), Decreto n.º 4.377, de 13 de setembro de 2002. Available online: http://www.planalto.gov.br/ccivil_03/decreto/2002/d4377.htm.

Carneiro, S. (2002), 'A Batalha de Durban', *Revista de Estudos Feministas*, 10 (1): 209–14. https://doi.org/10.1590/S0104-026X2002000100014.

Carneiro, S. (2004), 'A Mulher Negra na Sociedade Brasileira: O Papel do Movimento Feminista na Luta Antirracista', in K. Munanga (ed), *História do Negro no Brasil, vol. 1, O Negro na Sociedade Brasileira: Resistência, Participação, Contribuição*, 1–142, Brasília: Fundação Cultural Palmares, MINC.

Cerqueira, D., ed (2021), *Atlas da Violência*, São Paulo: FBSP.

Ciampa, A. C. (2001), *A Estória de Severino e a História de Severina: Um Ensaio sobre a Psicologia Social*, São Paulo: Brasiliense.

Freire, P. ([1968] 2014), *Pedagogia do Oprimido*, São Paulo: Paz e Terra.

Freire, P. ([1975] 2021), *Ação Cultural para a Liberdade e Outros Escritos*, São Paulo: Paz e Terra.

Freire, P. (1979), *Conscientização: Teoria e Prática da Libertação: Uma Introdução ao Pensamento de Paulo Freire*, São Paulo: Cortez & Moraes.

Freire, P. ([1992] 2011), *Pedagogia da Esperança: Um Reencontro com a Pedagogia do Oprimido*, Rio de Janeiro: Paz e Terra.

Gonzalez, L. (2020), *Por um Feminismo Afro-Latino-Americano*, Rio de Janeiro: Zahar.

Jaspers, K. (1993) *Introdução ao Pensamento Filosófico*, trans. L. Hegenberg and O. S. Mota, São Paulo: Cultrix.

Lane, S. M. (1984), 'O Processo Grupal', in S. M. Lane and W. Codo (eds), *Psicologia Social: O Homem em Movimento*, 78–98, São Paulo: Brasiliense.

Leontiev, A. (1978), *O Desenvolvimento do Psiquismo*, Lisboa: Horizonte Universitário.

Macedo, E. (2015), 'Violência e Violências sobre as Mulheres: Auscultando Lugares para uma Democracia "Outra" Mais Autêntica', in T. Brabo (ed), *Mulheres, Gênero e Violência*, 15–35, Marília: Oficina Universitária, São Paulo: Cultura Acadêmica.

Martin-Baró, I. (1989), *Sistema, Grupo y Poder: Psicologia Social desde Centroamérica*, San Salvador: UCA.

Melo, D. M. (2021), 'À Espera de um Observatório dos Feminicídios: Um Estudo da Atual Infraestrutura de Dados no Brasil à Vista da Obrigação de Transparência Ativa', *Anais de Artigos Completos do VI CIDH Coimbra 2021*, (8): 351–61.

Mészáros, I. (2002), *Para Além do Capital: Rumo a uma Teoria da Transição*, trans. S. Lessa and P. C. Castanheira, São Paulo: Boitempo.

Oliveira, B. (2005), 'A Dialética Do Singular, Particular, Universal', in. A. A. Abrantes, N. R. Silva and S. F. Martins (eds), *Método Histórico Social na Psicologia Social*, 25–51, Petrópolis: Vozes.

Saffioti, H. (1978), *Emprego Doméstico e Capitalismo*, Petrópolis: Vozes.

Santos, N. S. (2021), *Tornar-se Negro*, Rio de Janeiro: Zahar.

Vygotski, L. S. (2000), *Obras Escogidas: Problemas del Desarrollo de la Psique*, tomo III, trans. L. Kuper, Madrid: Visor.

Waiselfisz, J. J. (2015), *Mapa da Violência 2015: Homicídio de Mulheres no Brasil*, Brasília: FLACSO.

PART FOUR

Immersion in Freire's Thought and Educational Biographic Subjectivities

CHAPTER EIGHT

Revisiting an Educational Path Enlightened by Paulo Freire

Laura Fonseca

CIIE – Centre for Research and Intervention in Education of the Faculty of Psychology and Education Sciences, University of Porto, Portugal[1]

This text reflects upon an educational journey whose contours have challenges and potential. Scientific writing is complex because it confronts feelings of suffering related to the desire for satisfaction and pleasure arising from the creative energy of production/expression. When writing has the lived experience as an object, the task becomes riskier, as it deals with the subjectivity of the insight and the problem of escaping the *composition* of a story with some *comfort of oneself* (Summerfield 2000).

Subjectivity refers to the unique view of a subject. His or her story and experience define the ways in which he or she views the world and builds his or her own specific expectations about it.

Aware of this complexity, the option for (im)personal autobiography or socio-biography encompasses the potential of experience and the appreciation of both the processes of time and social power in our biographies. It is crucial 'not to waste the potential of the experience in the production of knowledge and learning of the subjects' (Torres 2001: 236).[2] This dual focus of indexing the social to the biographical, following Ferrarotti (1983), constitutes a heuristic and creative *milieu* that is socially and theoretically relevant to illuminate human action and the simultaneous understanding of the singular dimension of lived experience and the construction of collective and educational problems.

Heuristic refers to the mental shortcut people commonly use to simplify problems and avoid cognitive overload. This allows people to reach reasonable conclusions/solutions to complex problems.

Private and singular, plural and public, this writing evokes memories and personal experiences embedded in milestones and times of collective history, speaking of 'a common world' (Freire 1972: 17) through regularities and realities that will certainly be of interest to public education.

The socio-historical educational periodization was detailed in previous work (Fonseca 2017) and brings crucial dimensions to the dialogue. The **empirical dimension** takes the lived experience spanning almost five decades (1968–2014) between socio-educational practices and contexts – as an activist and/or professional teacher, social worker or educational academic; a path involved with reading and social transformation of the world (Freire 1972) of children, young people and adults, in projects, communities, public and private institutions, civic associations, and/or (inter)national organizations. The empirical support revisits memories, covering notes, texts produced and published individually or collectively, or comments made by colleagues/experts in the educational sociological field (Araújo 2015; Vieira 2004).

Reflexively, the **theoretical dimension** is inscribed in sociological research interests and pedagogies of social transformation – theorizations and methodologies with socially disadvantaged subjects who claim or desire change – in villages and urban environments, young or older, with social, ethnic, gender, class and sexual diversity.

This approach allowed the reconstitution of contexts, actions and concepts, identifying the presence of five educational waves that cross formal, non-formal and informal education, in which Freire's place is retained and named: 1968–April 1974 – education as social resistance; from 1974 – education as a political, cultural practice; 1980 – education as a practice for extending social rights and educational diversification; 1990 – youth education, European openings, and educational differentiation and scientificity; 2000–2014 – education and calls for the extension of citizenship to all people and spheres of life. (To further this discussion, please see the book in the series, 'Freire and Environmentalism: Ecopedagogy' by Greg William Misiaszek [2023], in which the author delves, in part, into various aspects of planetary citizenship.)

Lenses for structuring *scientificity*: Approximations and distances with Freire

Scientificity is used here to report to science as *in process* construction by the subject, shifting away from a view of science as a packed, ready to go (finished) set of objective knowledge.

The text is based on a powerful source of knowledge that takes advantage of human 'experience credentials', allowing reflection on everyday life, meanings and positions of subjects. Experience becomes a *source of knowledge and learning* for those who speak and those who know (Torres 2001). Experience constitutes the first central theoretical and methodological axis – a seminal place that reveals structures, ideologies and power relations; it allows *context*, human action and subjectivity to be summoned. In addition, taking advantage of the experience enables the 'political project of social criticism' because it identifies injustices and 'damage', whose sources are located in institutions and social relations. Moreover, it proposes directions for institutionally oriented action to change it (Young 2003).

Two senses are evoked to think of experience as a political project: a source of knowledge of undeniable primary value obtained first-hand, directly and without mediation; a *knowledge of trust*, which places the oppressed subjects at the centre of knowledge; it is important for subjects because it is knowledge about their own experience – an *authentic representation of themselves* (Young 1990). However, what counts as experience is neither self-evident nor straightforward; it requires fine instruments and clarity on what counts as knowledge and who makes that determination (Scott 1992). Recognizing the experience–knowledge connections requires generating analytical categories that facilitate the transition to scientific knowledge and practice (Araújo et al. 2002) and social action.

A second axis is the notion of **subject** – individual, social and historical, not simply psychological (Fonseca 2008, 2009; Touraine 1998) – central to the social science of transforming education: a subject constituted by social experiences and subjectivities, lived singularly; *constituted and affected* socially and culturally in context. The **educational subject** emerges as a source of political and scientific 'knowledge', 'learning', 'challenge/opportunity'; the possibility of *registering* and *naming* oppression and *pointing out* transformation by incorporating *pragmatic contexts of meaning* (Young 1990).

Each subject is the site of a range of possible forms of subjectivity – the dual notion of subject (subject and agent), which is central to understanding *oppression* and *autonomy* in Freire. Freire's transformative education has also been accentuated by feminist science, attributing political meaning to women as subject(s) in their plurality of voices and meanings, which criticize and progressively find and assert themselves in a *serial* collective subject (Young 2003).

A third axis is **oppression/oppressed**, central to *Pedagogy of the Oppressed* (Freire 1972) and seminal in my career, later reinterpreted with feminist contributions, particularly by Iris Young (2000). I retain Freire's notion of the oppressed as someone who lives in conditions of oppression – the socialization with codes of material and ideological perception of two social places, the oppressor and the oppressed. *Structural oppression* (Young 2000) densifies and makes Freire's approach even more complex. It focuses on five faces of oppression that act over certain groups, jointly or autonomously: *exploitation, marginalization, lack of power, cultural imperialism* and *violence*. It is an interesting approach to focus on the forms and suffering of oppressed individuals/groups who experience one or more (visible or discreet) forms of oppression under various combinations or intensities, paying attention to the discourses, experiences or cultural texts that reveal differences (Young 2000).

The fourth axis is related to *social justice* – a notion challenged in contact with Freire and acquired greater density in the 2000s by surpassing one-dimensionality and homogeneity. While historically the concept had a connotation with moral ethics, it was later seen predominantly in the redistributive dimension of linear 'access' to workers' social rights (the 1970s and 1980s). In the 2000s, a more critical form emerged, structurally more nuanced with feminist contributions (Lister, Young, Fraser, etc.). Thus, in the wake of the important educational work of Lynch and Lodge (2002), I argued for (Fonseca 2009) a **multidimensional social justice** approach to analyse the field of educational policies. This approach is articulated in four spheres: *redistribution* *policy* (access to educational goods, sources and resources); *recognition policy* (culturally and symbolically based systems of respect for differences); *policy of power and participation* (relations of the absence of power and decision-making; space for participation, autonomy and human action); and *policy of care* (need, right and responsibility of all to care and be cared for, attention and love in life and public policies).

Changes, debates, calls, and educational waves: The periodization hypothesis

1968–74 – Adult education as a practice of resistance with conscientization

The first educational wave concerns my journey from age sixteen as a student and young adult activist towards the educational world during the *Estado Novo* until April 1974. It addresses two directions, side by side, locally and temporally. The first is children's education as a young adult attending the training course and later teaching at the primary level (1968/9–1971/3). The training was built in silence and far from active movements and pedagogies. The perspective conveyed was one of *banking education* (Freire 1972), the instrumental instruction, and moralization of customs, subjects and communities.

Estado Novo was the dictatorial, authoritarian, autocratic and corporatist state political regime that existed in Portugal for forty-one years, from the approval of the Portuguese Constitution of 1933 until its overthrow by the revolution of April 25, 1974.

Banking education is a form of so-called education that builds on the transmission of knowledge. Teachers are seen as knowledgeable subjects and students as ignorant objects. The role of the teacher is to actively deposit his or her knowledge on passive students who receive it like banks receive money.

The **second** direction is that **non-formal adult education** goes against the grain. This work of 'problematizing education' is carried out under great moral and political pressure and control. It is clandestine, with adults at night, like *militant activism* committed to creating resistant awareness and change in the rural (semi-industrial) adult community in a situation of deep poverty and backwardness. The task is to raise literacy/awareness under the influence of radical progressive Christian ideas based on *Education as the Practice of Freedom* (Freire 1967) and the *Pedagogy of the Oppressed* (Freire 1972). It occurs in a closed community, under threat from the International and State Defence Police (PIDE) and local and national power hierarchies – political, religious and familial.

Post-1974 – Education as a practice of freedom *and the democratic, revolutionary, cultural struggle*

This wave contains milestones and changes from a political, educational and biographical point of view. It is inscribed in the revolutionary period of the 25th of April and then of constitutional 'normalization'. The narrator's journey is marked by the abandonment of teaching and the attendance of the higher education course of social work (1972–6) to emphasize the social dimension of educational action among groups with less power. With the involvement in the revolutionary democratic construction that the 25th of April fostered, the path is marked by educational and cultural intervention in three contexts: formal education, with the commitment to renewing the effervescent academic life of the course I attended, and the participation in the (inter)university struggle; and informal and non-formal education in the formation and articulation of cultural initiatives of popular education, together with popular organizations, such as:

(i)   with women, supporting the creation of a cooperative of women embroiderers (Braalcoop) accompanied by literacy processes, as a space to support participation in this self-managed collective (academic internship);

(ii) action in popular organizations in rural areas, in a factory and a neighbourhood in the city of Porto, in adult literacy teams;

(iii) participation in the constitution/training of a training structure for adult education trainers, guided by Brazilian educators close to Freire (Augusto Boal, among others). This was a space to learn/discuss pedagogy and methodological literacy tools in carefully and culturally localized and unique processes. The narrative emerges as learning and transformative educational action based on literacy and broad cultural dynamization processes – action framed by the Centre for Studies, Education and Culture (CEEC), a cultural collective autonomous of political power and parties.

The 1980s – Education as a social and institutional practice *for the extension of social rights and educational diversification*

In this phase of social and democratic 'normalization' in the 1980s, my educational work appeared above all in a professional context, in a Private Institution of Social

Solidarity (IPSS) for the social protection of children in a neighbourhood of the historic centre, where people were not provided with dignifying life conditions, and where I had previously participated in literacy processes. The experiential narrative emerged under the impulse of a strong technical and professional commitment to *social responsibility* in extending and applying social rights among socially marginalized and unprotected communities. I mobilized myself to expand my technical and scientific competencies by enrolling in a degree in educational sciences – in the interface between educational knowledge, qualification of professionals and social achievements. An excerpt/commentary by Helena Araújo (2015) on my professional work and the interlocution of this experience as a student is called for.

> In 1987, we saw her enroll in the degree in educational sciences [...], very much focused on the training/education of professionals with intervention in school and non-formal educational contexts [...]. Between 1981 and 1991, she coordinated the Centro Social da Sé Porto [...] she directed a set of equipment, services, and 'social responses' and conceived and animated several projects for children, youth, and elderly people, adjusted to 'needs' and 'rights' [...], initiatives with unemployed young people, [...] with women's groups, support for the elderly, in the Fight Against Poverty Programs [...] – 1989 to 1991 [...] a relevant, informed and critical interlocutor.

A notion of *social/educational responsibility* towards 'protected subjects' emerged, focused on expanding and qualifying the institutions' human resources as part of the awareness of their place in the realization of social rights (Welfare State) in the re/qualification of welcoming physical spaces; and the redefinition of the institutional place of assistance as a place of social and educational protection.

The 1990s – Non-formal youth education, European openings, educational differentiation, and scientificity

The path was marked by the professional expansion of the previous phase, followed by changes in my professional and educational trajectory. I dedicated my energy to capturing European impulses, resources and dynamics, participating in the Fight against Poverty and Petra programme – an exciting and creative phase in initiatives. Particularly noteworthy was the work within the scope of the project 'Com os Jovens da Sé' (With the *Sé* Youth) and in training/follow-up and coordination of various institutional action teams in coordination with the community. From here came the stimulus to produce various texts and academic research, the participation in pioneering research related to children/young people's experience of access to education, considering conditions of class, gender, ethnicity, age, etc., inserted in the research collective 'Novos Olhares, Reivindicações Antigas' (New Looks, Old Claims). Secondly, I should highlight a substantive change – leaving the Social Centre, joining the Regional Centre for Social Security in Porto, and teaching in education at the Instituto Superior de Serviço Social in Porto.

Thirdly, I would like to highlight the entry into the master's degree in education and social change, which culminated in the research 'Born and Bred in the Sé: Female Paths and Subjectivities in Education' (which gave rise, in 2001, to the book *Culturas Juvenis, Experiências e Subjectividades na Educação das Raparigas*–Youth Cultures, Experiences and Subjectivities in Girls' Education). This work was commented on as follows:

Perhaps one of the most important dimensions of this work lies in the deconstruction [...] of representations commonly constructed about the families of the popular classes of [...] neighborhoods [in lack of dignifying life conditions].

Contrary to the belief in the precariousness, disruption, and instability of family ties, the [...] study reveals that, as in society at large, there is a diversity of types of families [...] where female support appears as [...], decisive in consolidating lasting affective support aided, to a large extent, by 'neighborhood or kinship relations' (p. 196).

(Vieira 2004: 1214)

In a context in which academic research was beginning to gain momentum in Portugal (entrance to the EU), the contributions of feminist pedagogies, cultural studies and gender studies helped to broaden thinking by enriching Freire's pedagogies. There was openness to new horizons – multiculturalism, difference, class, women, children, youth, etc. – and awareness of the value of cultural rights, an issue that would be expanded in the 2000s.

The 2000s – Education and calls for the extension of citizenship to everyone and in all spheres of life

The last educational wave took place mainly in the 2000s. The academic world marked my path as a professor at the Faculty of Psychology and Education Sciences of the University of Porto in various subjects at undergraduate, master's and doctoral levels and as a researcher in the field of gender, youth, culture and citizenship studies, at the Centre for Research and Intervention in Education (CIIE). In addition to teaching and participating in research and intervention projects, there was an emphasis on the doctoral research 'Vozes, Silêncios e Ruídos na Educação Escolar das Raparigas Ciganas e Payas' concluded in 2006, and revised and published under the title 'Social Justice and Education: Voices, Silences and Noise in the Schooling of Roma and Paya Girls' (2009). I also produced texts that came to be included in what I named 'Education of Girls on the Threshold of the Twenty-First Century'. This was a period with the brand of cultural rights of youth citizenship and pedagogical rights at the intersection with socially vulnerable groups. Educational scientificity, linked to (inter)national research projects, marked the educational paths of this decade.

Between 2007 and 2011, I coordinated a research collective, 'Sexualidades, Juventude e Gravidez Adolescente a Noroeste de Portugal' (Sexualities, Youth and Adolescent Pregnancy in North-Western Portugal; Fonseca, Araújo and Santos 2012; Santos, Fonseca and Araújo 2012) that related educational policies and practices, health and diversity, and sexual and intimate citizenship. The collective reflected on the sexual cultures of students and young dropouts. The social responsibility of social and educational institutions towards *educational subjects*, often constituted as mere *protected subjects*, was questioned. Under the lens of the rights of sexual citizenship and intimate citizenship, we related redistribution, recognition, and care and solidarity in the face of social and educational subjects. Feminist and post-structuralist debates were central to this individual and collective deepening. Science and society are open to research in basic and secondary schools and other life spaces. The thought produced refers to the experience and the theoretical field. In the wake of critical theory, Freire's praxis is a theoretical and epistemological reference for thinking about social transformation through education. Freire's pedagogy is taken in terms of diversity awareness in the heterogeneous educational public space.

Room of Paulo Freire's thought in this path? Some points

This educational biography of nearly five decades shows a renewed awareness of the strength and preponderance of Freire's thought. The author's educational radicalism occupies an unavoidable place in training, in this individual historical time, and in the world as an inexhaustible source of inspiration and clairvoyance. Freire emerges as the most influential theorist of critical liberating education (Weiler 2004). But 'the goals of liberation or opposition in the face of oppression have not always been easy to understand or achieve' (92). This unique journey shows possible readings of this educational and historical time's dimensions, practices, policies, and important thoughts. Since the 1960s, Freire's teachings have marked the transformative quest of education and pedagogy as a *practice of freedom and autonomy*. They are present (i) when thinking about a resistant and conscientious education of the adult population through the novelty and charm of the readings, in the group discussions of educators on liberating pedagogy and praxiological requirements of the literacy method of learning to read life, in a locally situated exploration.

Praxeology is the science that studies human action. It relates to praxis (the dialogue between action and reflection on action) (Freire, 1972).

(ii) in the interest reiterated by subjects in situations of oppression/marginalization and the search for their involvement in individual/social transformation; working alongside rural–industrial men and women learners of literacy, workers and poor embroiderers in rural–industrial environments or in factories and neighbourhoods in the city that did not ensure dignifying life conditions; and (iii) in academic work with students, in which teaching tries to be praxis, in the choice of objects of study and methodologies resourcing to 'culture circles' – qualitative, inductive, biographical, ethnographic methodologies, action–research, conversations and group discussion, content analysis, construction of biographies, etc.; in the experiences of the professional relationship, of activism or scientificity, carrying the brand and perspectives – justice, social responsibility, autonomy, freedom, hope, love, participation and simultaneous transformation of educators, students and social realities.

Freire was present (i) in the 1970s, in the 'revolutionary' work involving the participation of different oppressed groups in a self-managed and autonomous action (production and commercialization cooperatives), in cultural work in education and popular struggle collectives; (ii) in the 1980s and 1990s, in the transformation and appropriation of the institutional public sphere, applying the broadening of social rights – implying equality and policies of difference and the presence of different social subjects. Despite this, the educational action appears to be predominantly focused on adult-centric citizenship, silencing children's citizenship; and (iii) in the 2000s, in the teaching professionalism and socio-educational scientificity that brought with it the challenges and heritage of Freire's praxis – an essential dialectical interconnection of theory and practice – in the causes of equality and citizenship, expansion to new projects and educational subjects: children, young people, women, Roma and sexualities. This is now challenged by the structuring contributions of feminist thinking from political and educational philosophy and some (post)modern educational thinking.

Notes

1   Acknowledgements: This work is also supported by the Portuguese government, through the Foundation for Science and Technology, IP (FCT), under the multi-year funding awarded to CIIE (grants no. UIDB/00167/2020 and UIDP/00167/2020).
2   See also Freire (1972); Plummer (1990); Stanley (1992); Araújo (1990, 2000); Araújo et al. (2002); Fonseca (2001, 2009); Fonseca and Santos (2015).

References

Araújo, H. C. (1990), 'Procurando as Lutas Escondidas através das Histórias de Vida', *Cadernos de Consulta Psicológica*, (6): 33–40.

Araújo, H. C. (2000), *Pioneiras na Educação, as Professoras Primárias na Viragem do Século 1870–1933*, Lisboa: IIE.

Araújo, H. C. (2015), *Diálogos com Laura Fonseca e a sua Contribuição para as Ciências da Educação/Ciências Sociais*, Porto: FPCEUP, 20 March.

Araújo, H. C., L. Fonseca, M. J. Magalhães and C. Leite (2002), 'Em busca da Interculturalidade e *Mulheres Ciganas e Padjas na Educação*', *Ex-aequo*, (7): 149–61.

Ferrarotti, F. (1983), *Histoire et Histoires de Vie*, Paris: Livrairie des Méridiens.

Fonseca, L. (1995), 'Nadas e Criadas na Sé: Em Busca de um Lugar para si Próprias', MA diss., Faculdade de Psicologia e de Ciências da Educação, Universidade do Porto, Portugal.

Fonseca, L. (2001), *Culturas Juvenis, Percursos Femininos, Experiências e Subjetividades na Educação de Raparigas*, Oeiras: Celta.

Fonseca, L. (2008), 'Transições à Entrada do Século XXI: Vozes, Percursos e Biografias Escolares de Jovens Ciganas e Payas', *Educação, Sociedade & Culturas*, (27): 51–72.

Fonseca, L. (2009), *Justiça Social e Educação: Vozes, Silêncios e Ruídos na Escolarização de Raparigas Ciganas e Payas*, Porto: Afrontamento.

Fonseca, L. (2017), 'Vaguear por Práticas, Lembranças, Textos e Comentários de um Percurso Educacional: O que é Crítico e Iluminações de Paulo Freire', in E. Macedo (ed), *Ecos de Freire e o Pensamento Feminista*, 107–36, Porto: Livpsic.

Fonseca, L. and S. Santos (2015), *Sexualidades, Gravidez e Juventude: Relações Sociais e Educativas*, Porto: Afrontamento.

Fonseca, L., H. C. Araújo and S. Santos (2012), 'Sexualities, Teenage Pregnancy and Educational Life Histories in Portugal: Experiencing Sexual Citizenship?', *Gender and Education*, 24 (6): 647–64.

Freire, P. (1967), *Educação como Prática da Liberdade*, Rio de Janeiro: Paz e Terra

Freire, P. (1972), *Pedagogia do Oprimido*, Porto: Edições Afrontamento.

Lynch, K. and A. Lodge (2002), *Equality and Power in Schools: Redistribution, Recognition and Representation*, London and New York: Routledge Falmer.

Misiaszek, G. W. (2023), *Freire and Environmentalism: Ecopedagogy*, London: Bloomsbury Academic. https://www.bloomsbury.com/us/freire-and-environmentalism-9781350292116/.

Plummer, K. (1990), *Documents of Life: An Introduction to the Problems and Literature of a Humanistic Method*, London: George Allen and Unwin Hyman.

Santos, S., L. Fonseca and H. C. Araújo (2012), 'Sex Education and the Views of Young People on Gender and Sexuality in Portuguese Schools', *Educação, Sociedade & Culturas*, (35): 29–44.

Scott, J. (1992), *Feminists Theorize the Political*, London and New York: Routledge.

Stanley, L. (1992), 'On Auto/biography in Sociology', *Sociology*, 27 (1): 41–52.

Summerfield, P. (2000), 'Dis/composing the Subject Intersubjectivities in Oral History', in T. Cosslett, C. Lury and P. Summerfield (eds), *Feminism and Autobiography: Texts, Theories, Methods*, 91–106, London and New York: Routledge.

Torres, C. A. (2001), *Democracia, Educação e Multiculturalismo*, Petrópolis: Vozes.

Touraine, A. (1998), 'Sociology without Society', *Current Sociology*, 46 (2): 119–43. https://doi.org/10.1177/0011392198046002008.

Vieira, M. M. (2004), 'Laura Pereira da Fonseca, Culturas Juvenis, Percursos Femininos: Experiências e Subjectividades na Educação das Raparigas', *Análise Social*, 38 (169): 1212–15.

Weiler, K. (2004), 'Freire e uma Pedagogia Feminista da Diferença', *Ex-aequo*, (7): 85–98.

Young, I. (1990), *Throwing Like a Girl and Other Essays in Feminist Philosophy and Social Theory*, Bloomington and Indianapolis, IN: Indiana University Press.

Young, I. (2000), *La Justicia y la Política de la Diferencia*, Valencia: Universitat de València: Ediciones Cátedra.

Young, I. (2003), 'Corpo Vivido vs Género: Reflexões Sobre Estrutura Social e Subjectividade', *Labrys, Estudos Feministas*, (3). https://www.labrys.net.br/labrys3/web/bras/young1.htm

CHAPTER NINE

Paulo Freire, Women's Emancipation and Liberating Education

Arilda Ines Miranda Ribeiro and Elaine Gomes Ferro

Introduction

Paulo Freire's philosophy is highly regarded in popular education; however, the range of his reflections allows for an analytical adoption of his writings by other fields of knowledge. In this sense, it is relevant to advance that the starting point of this text is to reflect on the potential contributions of Freire's thought to women's emancipation (liberation) in articulation with the notion of liberating education.

The first section of this chapter highlights the essential elements of Freire's thought by linking it to the possibility of women's emancipation through liberating education. The second presents a brief report of experience referring to the memories of Professor Arilda Ines Miranda Ribeiro, a former student of Freire, with the spotlight on her impressions about the periods when she was the educator's apprentice. By narrating her unique experience, this educator presents evidence of Freire's praxis and the importance of such accumulated experience throughout her intellectual emancipation.

It is worth highlighting that in addition to his theoretical and methodological contributions, Freire can also be considered a reference for optimism, solidarity, ethical commitment and activism, which are essential elements for women's struggles.

Oppressed women and education for freedom

In his work *Pedagogy of the Oppressed*, Paulo Freire emphasizes that even though the human being is an unfinished self, our vocation is aimed at humanizing; however, given the conditions of injustice, oppression, exploitation and violence to which humanity is exposed, this process would end, and both men and women would be dehumanized instead of humanized. For Freire, the way out would be the struggle of the oppressed with the oppressor to restore humanity in both: 'Those who oppress, exploit and violate, because of their power, cannot have, in this power, the force of liberation of the oppressed or themselves' (Freire [1968] 2014: 41, our translation).

Even though in this latter statement, Freire acknowledges the situation of oppression of humanity in general, it is worth reflecting that, in addition to the oppression, exploitation and violence shared with men, women are also exposed to what can be named as another form of dehumanization: the sexism to which they are subjected in different forms.

If humanity finds the necessary strength for its liberation in the struggle of the oppressed, likewise, women who acknowledge this double oppression can find the necessary conditions for the statement of their humanizing.

For this educator from the state of Pernambuco, for historical reasons and especially for preserving the *status quo*, the oppressor would never be able to free the oppressed; thus, it is up to the oppressed to organize themselves to transform their history (Freire [1968] 2014). Therefore, it is worth emphasizing that the history of achievement of rights, especially women's, shows that the oppressed and not the oppressors struggled in favour of women's emancipation.

Freire points out that the process of dehumanization in society cannot be faced deterministically since it is not a result of fate but of unfair orders through which the oppressor violates the oppressed. This means that by emphasizing the non-naturalness of such a perverse process, the author indicates that overcoming oppression and gaining freedom are also possible. For him, freedom 'is an achievement, not something granted, requiring a permanent search. [...] No one has the freedom to be free: on the contrary, we struggle for it precisely because we do not have it' (Freire [1968] 2014: 46).

In the field of women's emancipation, some discourses have opposed the causes of the feminist movement (Perrot 1988) by arguing, among other factors, that women cannot and/or should not occupy the 'place' that men have historically occupied (Lagrave 1991). Considering Freire's thought, it is worth noting that this argument does not align with the struggle for women's emancipation. That is, as Freire suggests, the oppressed must not aim at liberation to occupy the place before occupied by their oppressor. By seeking freedom, Freire explains, the oppressed also seek liberation from their oppressors and the consequent restoration of humanity in both (Freire [1968] 2014).

Thus, overcoming sexism, in the scope of the oppressor–oppressed relationship in Freire, does not suggest implementing a feminist 'dictatorship' since women do not seek freedom simply to subdue and/or oppress the opposite sex. Even though women are the main victims of sexist oppression, they are not the only ones since the ultimate achievement of women's emancipation provides for an inclusive liberation of men, who also, to a greater or lesser extent, end up as victims of the oppression originating in the patriarchal society (Saffioti 2004).

For Freire, the main emancipatory route is to work with the oppressed so that he or she becomes aware of the condition of dominance in which they live. For this purpose, they need a permanent formative process carried out according to an effective movement of popular participation. For the author, education is essential in overcoming oppression and alienation, and it aims to emancipate and free both men and women (Freire [1967] 2014).

Even though Freire's work is not directly related to the causes of feminist struggles, his reflections on liberating education corroborate studies that analyse educational elements, such as a strategy for feminist action. Freire's limited writing is worth mentioning, specifically about feminism and/or social–gender relations. He was even criticized by feminists for employing patriarchal language in his writing, using the universal masculine mainly in his early works. These criticisms specifically referred to the book *Pedagogy of the Oppressed*, his best-known work. In a later work, Freire ([2001] 2014: 327) stated:

> It is with great satisfaction that I admit that my engagement with feminist movements enabled me to focus more accurately on gender issues. For this, I am indebted to North American feminists, who have drawn my attention on several occasions to gender discrimination. It was during the 1970s, after the publication of *Pedagogy of the Oppressed*, that I began to reflect more deeply and learn more systematically about the work of feminists.

However, by claiming education for men and women in favour of women's emancipation from a critical, democratic and popular perspective, feminism can find a motto for a liberating education in Freire's reflections.

For Freire, it is the society that shapes education according to its interests:

> It would be too naive to ask the ruling class in power to implement a kind of education that can work against it.

If education were allowed to develop without political oversight, this would bring endless problems for those in power.

(Freire and Shor 1986: 49, our translation)

In this sense, we can see that governments have acted tentatively towards including issues related to gender inequality in Brazilian school curricula, and the actions that have already been carried out have not yet been able to raise awareness of the problem.

Such a scenario of absence (or limited presence), especially of gender issues, suggests that, as Freire explains (Freire and Shor 1986), education is used by the ruling class as a tool of ideological control to preserve power and privileges. Thereby, it would be naive to believe that the oppressor class that makes use of 'sexist ideals' to their benefit, to a lesser or a greater extent, would prioritize issues involving inequality and gender identity in the curricula.

As analysed by Freire, the education planned by the oppressing class clearly aims to reproduce the ruling ideology. Thus, a counter-hegemonic education would be a denouncement and activism effort favouring the oppressed classes. Such a task cannot be proposed by those who oppress.

It must be fulfilled by those who dream of the reinvention of society, the recreation or reconstruction of society. So, it is up to those whose political dream is to reinvent society to occupy the space of the schools and the institutional space and uncover the reality hidden by the ruling ideology and the ruling curriculum.

(Freire and Shor 1986: 49)

This last excerpt reveals the revolutionary potential of Freire's educational project. Thus, based on this clarification, it is worth inferring that feminism finds a solid theoretical/ practical reflection in Freire's model to establish and/or plan/ organize actions to raise awareness regarding gender and inequality.

Paulo Freire and me: An apprentice

The following narrative illustrates the impact of the thought and image that Paulo Freire evoked. This reflective description reveals the influence exerted by Freire on the professional trajectory of a professor who studies social–gender relations:

My father, a sergeant in the Brazilian army during the military dictatorship, was sent to a different place every two years. My family and I would move from city to city until we ultimately settled in Campinas in 1975.

I went to a public high school between fifteen and seventeen years old. I chose the library science course at the Pontifícia Universidade Católica de Campinas, imagining I would have greater contact with the universe of books. At that time, I worked as a bank teller at the Bradesco Bank downtown. By the end of the day, I was tired and without showering, and would go straight to the university. Then, I decided to quit my job, gather my accumulated income and pursue a master's degree in the same area of library science. However, the course proved to be too technical. I almost abandoned the idea of continuing my studies when I decided to take an elective discipline, philosophical anthropology, taught by professor and poet Régis de Moraes. I decided to return to the undergraduate level and study philosophy. However, Régis, who was an educator, questioned my decision. Since I took the master's in library science, why not switch to philosophy applied to education? It would be more useful both to me and to society in general. Then, Professor Régis de Moraes advised me to attend some lessons by Professor Paulo Freire, who had recently arrived in Brazil after a forced exile, to see if I saw myself in education.

I decided to accept Professor Régis' suggestion. I started to be shy and afraid of his answer. I didn't know much about him. I met one of his students, Adriano Nogueira, who, due to his immediate empathy, helped me to approach him. Paulo Freire asked me to tell him what I had done in life so far. I spoke briefly about my father, the dictatorship, the changes, quitting the bank, taking the library science course, getting my master's degree, meeting Régis de Moraes and being referred to his lessons. After my narrative, in a sweet, easy voice, he looked me in the eyes and said: 'If you want to come and hear me and talk, come. Join us, students, journalists, workers, farmers, former seminarians, friends, and many others already here. There will be many! I will talk about that with you today: the strength of union!'

I was delighted by his ways, simplicity, clothes and even his sneakers – since I had only seen professors wearing shoes until then. The lessons followed. Every day, the narratives would move me. I learned so many new and interesting things! Having lived so many years abroad, he proudly kept his Northeastern accent. With it, he would slide in words that were active, reflexive, and filled with pedagogical experiences in a sweet and content manner. I had never seen someone talk so profoundly and calmly in academia. He would speak of his experiences abroad. His charisma and affection for Brazil were clear, especially his respect for the needy, the humble, and those who are not aware of the transforming strength that they have. As a good educator, he would leave the erudite discourse behind to 'talk' using simple and direct words. He would start from the educational reality imposed by the oppressors to the concrete reality of the oppressed. In his lessons, he would say that to know the reality as a political option aimed at liberation, we must know the ways of thinking and the actions of the popular groups. It is not by being concerned with oneself that one educates oneself; it is by being concerned with the world and being aware of what it is about. That is the true autonomy of the educator.

But in his reminiscences of exile, Freire would tell us how much he missed his homeland. He would long for the Northeastern food, his family, relatives, and buddies to chat to, his people's folklore, traditions and parties. He was exiled in 1964 and returned almost twenty years later. He led a private and distant life with his wife, Elza, and his children for quite a while. Catholic, he was considered atheist and subversive. Contradictorily, thanks to his Christian faith, he achieved shelter with the Catholic Church and the possibility of teaching adult literacy in the Ecclesial Base Communities worldwide.

Our lessons would always end around noon, and Paulo Freire would extend them by inviting us, as student–friends, to have lunch with him in places he would choose. Places that would remind him of his old days in Pernambuco. We once went to a truck driver's restaurant on the Anhanguera Highway to eat 'jabá' (jerked beef) with flour. Another time, he took us to a humble house near the old Campinas Bus Station, where a lady had a backyard with a dirt floor. Under a mango tree on a big table, we ate simple and trivial delicacies of Brazilian cuisine cooked on a wood-burning stove.

At these lunches, we would continue with our lessons. Or better, the practice of our theoretical lessons. In every gesture and every attitude, my colleagues and I were proving his reflections on how to treat the other, the 'being' as the other, with happiness and respect: Freire's altruism.

By the end of 1982, I tried to pursue a master's degree at UNICAMP (State University of Campinas), but I failed. I still didn't know enough to occupy one of its vacancies. I could not resist the opportunity to enroll as a special student and, once again, in Professor Paulo Freire's course.

I completed the master's degree in 1984, and he retired from UNICAMP in 1985 to live in São Paulo definitively after his wife, Elza, passed away. I met with Paulo Freire in later periods as a lecturer at congresses and scientific events. Those were good gatherings!

In 1988, I took my doctorate at the same Faculty of Education. In 1992, I started working as a professor at UNESP, State University Paulista Júlio de Mesquita Filho, the campus of Presidente Prudente, São Paulo. I taught many lessons over the twenty-four years, during which I imparted

FIGURE 9.1 *On Paulo Freire's right is Bernardo, his driver, and on his left is Neusa Alves from Bahia. Sitting (below Neusa Alves), Arilda Ribeiro. Truck Drivers' Restaurant, Anhanguera Highway – Campinas/SP (1982).*
Source: *Personal archive of Prof. Arilda Ines Miranda Ribeiro.*

the course on the history of education. I always mentioned him as an example of a great educator by his pedagogy of the oppressed.

I am grateful and proud of all I learned from him and my other professors. How lucky I was! As a woman and a scholar on the gender issue.

Final remarks

By way of an overview, we presented some elements of Paulo Freire's thoughts, attempting to link his ideas to the struggle for women's freedom. Thereby, we raised the hypothesis that education, from an emancipatory and liberating perspective, can empower women and strengthen the feminist movement based on its humanizing, transforming nature. Freire's thought also highlights that the greater awareness of reality and the more developed critical thought is, the greater the possibility of political actions favouring freedom.

The reflections presented indicate that the current awareness of the oppression experienced by women must be the starting point for achieving critical awareness. In the field of action, popular knowledge must be appreciated through a democratic educational process based on dialogue and mutual respect. Freire shows that no educational action must be imposed but rather built through the direct participation of all those involved, which he expressed in his practice, as is clear in Professor Arilda's narrative experience as a student of his courses at UNICAMP (State University of Campinas).

Finally, establishing a dialogue between the knowledge accumulated within the feminist movements and Freire's pedagogy is a challenge and an important strategy for politicizing formative women's actions.

Tribute (In Memoriam)

Jorge Luís Mazzeo Mariano (1986–2023)

Jorge Luís Mazzeo Mariano was a Brazilian artist, teacher and researcher, whose research focused mainly on themes about the history of Brazilian education and women's History, gender studies, school culture and oral history.

Professor Jorge was born in the city of Mococa, in the interior of the state of São Paulo, on April 1, autumn of 1986.

In 2008, he graduated in Pedagogy at Universidade Estadual Paulista Júlio de Mesquita Filho – Unesp, Presidente Prudente campus. In his rich academic experience, he also participated in the student movement, finding himself in the field of research on the history of education and gender studies, having published his first scientific article during this period, in addition to having participated in his first scientific events.

In 2009, Jorge enrolled in the Master's Program in Education at the Federal University of São Carlos – UFSCar, in the research line of history, philosophy and sociology of education, receiving his master's degree in 2011. In 2012, at the age of twenty-five, he married Elaine Gomes Ferro, then a master's student.

During the same year he completed his master's degree, he was accepted for a doctorate in education at Unesp (Presidente Prudente campus), under the guidance of Professor Dr Arilda Inês Miranda Ribeiro, and defended his thesis in 2016. After completing his doctorate, between 2017 and 2018, he completed his postdoctorate.

The educator also has several publications in Brazil and abroad, in addition to having participated in main scientific events in the areas of education, gender and history of education, at national and international levels. In 2018, at the age of thirty-two, Jorge joined the Federal University of Mato Grosso do Sul – UFMS (Pantanal Campus) as an assistant professor. In parallel with his brilliant academic performance, he continuously produced a series of artistic works, such as drawings, paintings and engravings. Self-portraits, political themes, existential provocations and academic life stood out among the subjetcs of his body of work.

In 2022, professor and artist Jorge Luís was diagnosed with advanced stage cancer and, despite having fought bravely, unfortunately passed away prematurely, in the fall of 2023, exactly sixteen days after turning thirty-seven years old, in the city of Campo Grande, after a five-month battle against a rare and aggressive tumour.

Due to his illness, unfortunately, Professor Jorge was unable to contribute to this last work. This publication would certainly fill him with pride and satisfaction. An advocate for education, Professor Jorge dedicated his career to studying women's participation in teaching, with Paulo Freire being his academic, social and personal inspiration. He left behind an invaluable material and immaterial legacy.

We would like to express our gratitude and affection to Professor Jorge Luís.

Brazil, spring 2024

References

Freire, P. ([1967] 2014), *Educação como Prática da Liberdade*, 36th edn, Rio de Janeiro: Paz & Terra.

Freire, P. ([1968] 2014), *Pedagogia do Oprimido*, 57th edn, Rio de Janeiro: Paz & Terra.

Freire, P. ([2001] 2014), *Pedagogia dos Sonhos Possíveis*, Rio de Janeiro: Paz & Terra.

Freire, P. and I. Shor (1986), *Medo e Ousadia: O Cotidiano do Professor*, Rio de Janeiro: Paz & Terra.

Lagrave, R.-M. (1991), 'Uma Emancipação sob Tutela: Educação e Trabalho das Mulheres no Século XX', in G. Duby and M. Perrot (eds), *História das Mulheres no Ocidente: O Século XX*, Vol. 5, 505–43, Porto: Afrontamento.

Perrot, M. (1988), *Os Excluídos da História: Operários, Mulheres e Prisioneiros*, Rio de Janeiro: Paz & Terra.

Saffioti, H. B. (2004), *Gênero, Patriarcado, Violência*, São Paulo: Fundação Perseu Abramo.

INDEX

INDEX – FREIRE'S WORKS